D1525779

Robert Frost
Six Essays in Appreciation

For information address:
Stephen F. Austin State University Press
1936 North Street, LAN 203
Nacogdoches, TX 75962
sfapress@sfasu.edu

Distributed by Texas A&M University Press Consortium
tamupress.com

Book Design by Troy Varvel

LIBRARY OF CONGRESS CATALOGING-IN-PUBLICATION DATA

Kuzma, Greg
Robert Frost: Six Essays in Appreciation/Greg Kuzma 1st ed.

ISBN: 978-1-936205-71-4

Robert Frost
Six Essays in Appreciation

Greg Kuzma

Stephen F. Austin State University Press
2014

Dedicated to the family and
descendents of Robert Frost
whose sufferings permit
these poems to become ours.

The poems I write about in this book are not the usual ones. It may look like I have been overly perverse in choosing the strange and the lesser, and then have overreacted in praising them far beyond their desserts. This has not been my intention. The poems were not so much chosen as they drew me to themselves—they chose me, and I have been faithful to them as well as I am able. I do not pretend that I know of no finer poems written by Robert Frost—there are many as good as these here looked at, and maybe some that are better. Those "better," or more easily liked, or more ambitious in scope or length or voice, have long ago been spoken for, both by many fine readers and by Frost himself. To an extent I was after the poem less studied. Perhaps, after decades of neglect, "Birches" may again look new and fresh to some future reader.

My larger concern was for a kind of poem, a kind of poem "Hyla Brook" is. You can see for yourselves the kinds of poems I examine here, and draw your own conclusions about what they have in common. My sense is this—I found in "Hyla Brook," in "Mowing," and the other poems, poems splendidly evocative of real and physical things while, at the same time, not being programmatic about it. What I encountered reading Frost is what anyone finds, a poet of beautifully extreme self-awareness. He was, I think, (and became even worse at it) too smart for his own good. His famous guideline about surprise—none in the writer—none to the reader—is certainly operative. But we can honestly ask at what point the poet's surprise diverges from that of the reader. Too often the poet is far ahead of us, he having all the advantage on us of intention coupled with familiarity as to his ways of speaking and what troubles are brewing in his unconscious. Frequently his poems are jokes we arrive for a little too late, or they are lectures where the poet tries to appear spontaneous but still sounds studied and rehearsed. What I was looking for is the poem that is always at risk, and ends up more or less a lucky accident, where Frost and the language are too intent on what they are about, too occupied, too full of themselves, to have occasion to look back or ahead. The poems I love are the head-down poems—the poet in the thick of it, where what we get we almost didn't get at all, and each time to it, in the repeating, are surprised again, and glad.

Robert Frost may not have been all we'd hope for in a human being, all we'd like ourselves to be, but he was a supreme craftsman and a very daring writer. I think for the sheer joy being in the company of his language in such poems as I review here, there is no one more exciting in our century.

Additional Praise for *Robert Frost: Six Essays in Appreciation*

In his insighful and original readings of Frost, Greg Kuzma argues for "the poem that is always at risk" by looking closely at the music diction and syntax create. Kuzma explores, in accesible language, the "wonderful tension" in meter; he charts sound as they morph and reproduce across a poem; he demonstrates Frost's "essential reasonableness." These six essays model deep study and passionate engagement; I recommend them for anyone interested in Frost's achievement or in how we talk, think and write about lyric poetry.

—Robin Becker, author of *Tiger Heron*

A patient, knowledgeable, and ebullient exegete, Greg Kuzma guides the reader through the dense woods and meadows of six of Robert Frost's less well-known poems. Kuzma scrutinizes each poem with open mind, alert eye and ear, and loving criticism with a touch of asperity. He is wondrously indefatigable, turning over every line, like a farmer his furrow and an archeologist his site, unearthing and extracting valuable information from the surface of a poem—its sounds and images, its sequences of words and rhythms, its surprising reversals—down to a single syllable at bedrock. One takes away from Kuzma's zealous and engaging analyses of "Mowing" and the other five poems a deeper appreciation of Frost's crafty and complex art. Even the Yankee poet, notoriously stingy with praise, would have to admit that he learned much from Kuzma about how his poems stitched together words, tones, themes, and textures.

Herbert Leibowitz, author of *Something Urgent I Have to Say to You*

Table of Contents

Robert Frost's Ambitions in "Mowing"

Robert Frost's ambitions in "Mowing" are many. It is another of Frost's poems of field in which the dynamics of decision and finding are more important than any statement the poem may ultimately yield. Like all of Frost's greatest poems it is investigative, and it works toward a statement of vision. This poem's greatest virtue is in the testing it makes against limits—how far things can be pushed or pursued.

At times playful against the imagination of daydream and magic, "Mowing" asserts the primacy of the mind's fullest engagement when, aware of the dangers of numbing labor and the dangers of an abstracted rationalizing, it finds its firmest ground somewhere in between. Middle ground is always Frost country. We must define ourselves or we allow others to do it for us, which is to be a slave, in effect, and to define ourselves between alternatives, often extreme alternatives.

Sometimes boundaries are parts of camps, entrenchments, where possibility loses its elasticity and idea becomes formula, slogan, political platform or warcry. Frost begins on the edge of such a position, and he stays there grandly for a while, to savor the view, to taunt us with his loftiness.

> There was never a sound beside the wood but one,
> And that was my long scythe whispering to the ground.
> What was it it whispered? I knew not well myself;
> Perhaps it was something about the heat of the sun,
> Something, perhaps, about the lack of sound—
> And that was why it whispered and did not speak.
> It was no dream of the gift of idle hours,
> Or easy gold at the hand of fay or elf:
> Anything more than the truth would have seemed too weak
> To the earnest love that laid the swale in rows,
> Not without feeble-pointed spikes of flowers
> (Pale orchises), and scared a bright green snake.
> The fact is the sweetest dream that labor knows.
> My long scythe whispered and left the hay to make.

Frost's first line is splendidly bold. It proves the audacity Frost honored again and again in his work, and which he came to praise in people and himself. It is a line that is a partial lie, which seeks the truth, a raising of the voice so as to hear better the silence, a line weighted with and explained by history, and yet mere words in the mouth of one person, alone, amidst the mysteries. Like all of Frost's best lines it has a strong element of newness to it, and like some other lines it teeters on the brink of having too much to it, having gone too far. Right away it bears out the reason we return to Frost—for recklessness within tight confines, for fresh thought formed under pressure of its own making. Never a sound, he says: never a sound but one!

With Frost we learn early that the games he plays have few rest periods. Nor is there a warm up. Frost is busy from the start, and the power and eloquence with which he begins "Mowing" has such urgency to it, such an edge, that we feel as if we are thrown into the middle of something whose stakes are already set and high and whose action is already underway. Courage is its own accomplishment. Or audacity itself may win the day. Frost is not immune to the advantages of slow growth—in other poems he begins slowly and likes to dally or delay or go on detours, but he is most boldly himself in what he calls "the liberties he takes." Here the liberty taken is on behalf of exclusiveness. One sound, and one sound alone. What we get here is somewhat similar to the emphasis afforded the beginning syllables of "The Road Not Taken," where three of the first four syllables bear stress. Here in "Mowing," however, all the stress falls on "never," on the first half of the word. If it is not too much in imitation of the man let me assert that Never has a word had to bear such weight. Why should Frost choose to do this? Does he not, at the outset, overplay his hand, or bid too high. "Mowing" is one of those rare poems that begins with a deadly gambit, so risky that no amount of later proof or play can quite make up for the sense that we have been to the very edge. For some readers, perhaps, with such a beginning Frost simply can't in such a small space as remains in the sonnet justify this first line. Perhaps my sense that there is too much haste in some later lines comes from this.

The speaker is beside "the wood." He is where people have made a stand. He is at the edge of the clearing, a clearing made so that the sun come down and grow something other than tall spindly trees reaching for "a place in the sun." He is on ground cleared before, by labor such as this, by work done by others, and so his "never" speaks in tribute to that which is most human against the many other sounds, the sounds of nature. Frost is, here as always, after the human. The woods must not grow back, the human must stand itself apart. The first line is also, for those who find this poet overly smug and overly self-assertive, just the sort of thing he says too often for his own good or ours. To be insulated from so much is a fault, to hear only his own sound, to insist too much on his own voice, his own importance. But there is a need to seek for explanation within the special nature of the sort of work this is. This is a work poem, and Frost speaks through this kind of work. The poem keeps faithful to its particular scene. Cutting grass by hand scythe requires a certain strength, a rhythm, a back and forth movement in which the blade is brought in contact with the grass at the most efficient angle for cutting. Mowing is hard work, and it needs to be attended to with a keenness of body. It requires a discipline and skill not easy to come by. It has its aesthetics, its grace, its order and rhythm. Crucial to the meaning of the first line of Frost's poem is the insulating effect of the sound of the scythe for the mower doing the work. Working in grass the mower is immersed in the sound of his work as he does it, and is cut off from other sounds. To him there is no sound beyond his own, "never a sound beside the wood but one."

How much Frost is in the grip of this work is an important question. How much does he want to dramatize the reality of the mower. Sometimes when I read the poem I note the detachment of the speaker, and I can see how other readers find Frost rather idle in the poem, too speculative or talky, certainly more a poet than a worker. And the old criticism comes forth, that Frost exploits for the profit of poetry the work he never really gave himself to. But my feeling is that Frost is uncommonly sensitive to the experience he's writing about. For there is another dimension to the first line which is just as essential to its effect as any reliance on faith in Frost or lack of it. Frost is a metrical poet, sometimes by sheer will power—who holds out for meter and rhyme in the face of much pressure to do otherwise. Often the play of the syllables seems no more than play, a given imposition won without opposition. But here the tug of syllables, the rise and fall of meter, serves Frost well, serves even to validate the process of the work in that the work itself partakes of these movements. Reading the first line is like being present at the birth of the beat, to be privileged to feel where form and voice emerge as one. However else we wish to justify "never" in this context it's clear that the first line resolves itself in iambs. Is this the sound of the scythe? I think so. And I want to say too that Frost sets the scythe going with this first line, and that the pressure put on "never" and given back to us is that force that needs to be asserted so that the inertia of the object be overcome. Once set in motion the scythe continues, so that the first line then moves along with the smooth regularity of the labor. I use "assertion" for "exertion" here, the force that needs to be exerted I should have said, which is to show, however, how closely the work of the work and the work of the poem are one.

The sound of the scythe it turns out is present in abundance in "Mowing." The feel of the work is in the rhythm of the lines. One can almost hear Frost's question in line three— "What was it it whispered?"—answered in the second half of the line by his own not knowing under the spell of the scythe—"I knew not well myself." Line two is a wonderfully complex line for how its rhythm runs so counter to the rhythm with which line one ends: "And that was my long scythe whispering to the ground." Is this some counter-rhythm, the less predictable force of thought as measured against a regularity of movement identified as labor? Perhaps. Perhaps one may wish to set up opposing voices here the way Frost sets up two roads in "The Road Not Taken." Frost does, for all his loose talk of heat and silence and snakes and elves and gold, narrow down to fact and dream in line thirteen. Or to begin with there are two, the man who works the scythe and the scythe itself, attached, together, the one the mover the other the moved, scythe which whispers and the mower who would decode that whispering. Frost may also be playing here with background and foreground, what is conscious one time and then dims down and seems to move into context. The scythe is very much foregrounded in line 1, only to become subordinate by line 3 where Frost's urge to understand what is being whispered sets in motion another rhythm. In one scheme, line 1 remains quite neutral, almost in innocence. Sound is still fact, no more than fact. It is not until Frost gives a name to it, puts a word upon it, "whispering"—that Eden is violated. Line 1 is the pure voice of God (so much for our wonder at Frost's authority!)—and even line 2 with its "whispering" is more sound than sense. One plainly hears how appropriate a word it is for the situation if you have ever done the sort of work Frost writes about here. The blade moves down close upon the ground, brushing its blade parallel to the surface, the way we whisper by bringing our face close to someone's ear. That closeness is one dimension of this rightness, perhaps in itself a sufficient attraction to lock the word in place amidst other hissy words like shussing or hissing. (Had Frost chosen "hissing" instead, it's important to note, we'd have to worry about the snake and good and evil, with the mower the grim reaper variety.) Frost's choice of "whispering" is sheer genius, genius that shows off the poet's incredible resourcefulness but also the natural genius of the language itself. As the scythe moves through the air its width of blade makes a whirr in air, displacing air as it comes, sideways mostly, and this is expressed in the first syllable with its windy "wh" sound. Then, as the grass is struck, we get a new sound of sharp steel against hard cellulose and the stiffness of the grass, and so the sharp "s" sound comes into play. Finally, if this were not abundance enough, Frost carries the scythe through and upward out of the grass where the blade, having been struck, is set into the ring of its vibration. "Whispering" provides the "ring" in its last syllable.

"Whispering" is certainly the showcase word of the poem. All by itself it validates the effort—for poetry, if it can do anything, might give us back our language with new wonder in its powers. Frost's discovery of the wealth of the word in this context is an incredible find which cannot be too much emphasized. "Mowing" would be duly famous for it no matter what else Frost had tried to do. Such is the pleasure afforded by a good ear. Frost heard "whispering" into being—because he knows the work—the sound the work makes. I also like to think Frost *makes* the word as much as finds it, or that he could have assembled it out of its component parts and offered it for us as pure sound, purely the sound the scythe makes, its voice in the world. Let me also suggest that cousin to "whisper" is "never," from line 1, that "never" is antecedent. The "er" sound the words share is not particularly forceful in this poem, although Frost behaves as one obsessed by the sound in a later poem like "The Sound of Trees," also very much an ear poem. Frost begins like an owl or bat to zone in on the sound in "Mowing" but he gets distracted along the way by the more-substantial sound and accidental miracle of "whispering." What we get then is praise for Frost for the beguiling eloquence of "never," on one hand a totally gratuitous assertion, nearly all wind and pose, voice pushing for the pure joy of it, whose eloquence begets the marvelous accuracy of "whispering." Put another way—Frost takes the liberty to act like God, our one to talk of nevers, only to be overcome by the very earthly powers of the senses and find whispering in all its glory. So "Mowing" begins in ecstasy.

It is not easy to be done with these felicities. Happy accident and magic compound themselves, and "whispering" proves to be abundant beyond all suspicions. Scattered into component sounds, the "w" and "s" essentially (although the "per" achieves reincarnation twice in "perhaps"), Frost next works to work under the spell and to free himself from it.

> What was it it whispered? I knew not well myself;
> Perhaps it was something about the heat of the sun,
> Something, perhaps, about the lack of sound—
> And that was why it whispered and did not speak.

"What" and "was" and "whispered" and "well" and "was" and "why" and "whispered" again. And the "s" alone in "myself" and "perhaps" and "something" (twice) and "sun" and "sound" and "speak." And so on, into the next group of lines. So that even in a line where the iambic or anapestic rising meter is absent (and where the scythe is less present rhythmically), a line like "And that was why it whispered and did not speak"— the scythe persists in its consonance.

We could go on praising Frost's early accomplishment (and

I will) but all is not entirely well with this poem. The build-up Frost gives to the sound in the first line catches our attention, tunes our ears and makes us wonder what that sound might be, all to his advantage certainly, but I think it promises more than it delivers. When we get into the second line Frost furthers the introduction with a long run of heavily-stressed syllables (loud when spoken), a kind of "Ladies and Gentlemen, for your enjoyment, the great and powerful Oz, and so forth: 'And that was my long scythe...'" I'm overdoing this a little— "was" might well be less-stressed, or unstressed, keeping the iambic pattern established fairly well in the last two thirds of the first line. Just as easily, however, "was" can pick up the big stress on "never" in line 1 by virtue of its parallel positioning. "Was" is also the verb, and so is important, and is enhanced further through repetition—"was," after all, is the second word of the poem. And "was" also picks up attention as an alliterative word in the "wood but one" series which ended line one. Similar deliberations inform questions of emphasis for "my" and "long" or "that." "My" is a word we might want to limit a bit as a possessive pronoun and coming two syllables away from its noun, but "my" is exiting here for its surprise. To some extent, Frost's godlike overview of the universe in line one suggests an objectivity—we half expect Frost to overhear the sound and talk about its place in context or in history. But the "my" shatters that expectation and in doing so attracts our curiosity. It is not some *other* sound Frost overhears but a sound whose making *he* is responsible for. "Long" takes stress by contagion—"that" has it by virtue of position after the iambic run at the end of line one, "was" as indicated above, and "long" also because it falls in the place we expect the noun, and "scythe" receives stress as what might be first thought of as the long-awaited sound itself. But of course "scythe" is not the sound but the source of sound, and so having been drawn out here so far past metrical safety and iambic give and take we have to go one more syllable to the next word. To "whispering." To have gone so far, to have stretched our patience and our breath is a real achievement (Is this what Frost means by his famous "loose iambic"?—six stressed syllables in a row!). But with "whispering" we run out of breath. We run out for sure on the third syllable. And certainly we are relieved to get to the second syllable—the first of seven where we can release the tension. But maybe, by some wonderful luck, we even run out with the first syllable! What is a whisper after all but strong breathy talk without a volume of sound, words that hiss with breath but have none of the personal tone by which we recognize voices. To run out of breath on "whispering," or, rather, to run out of voice while keeping a modicum of breath acts out what the word says. We whisper it. The problem, however, is all the time trying to catch up with the poet. Frost has stretched our voices and his past the breaking point and at precisely the moment when we had expected he would be delivering the goods. The build-up is grand, the stretching is terribly exciting in that we don't know just how far this poet will reach, but the word is disappointing. So this is the great sound, is it? This whispering.

"Mowing" for some readers may not survive Frost's superhuman efforts in the first two lines. Even a sympathetic reader will note how the poem seems dispirited and slack afterwards, how it gets talky, almost apologetic, and how, after so much seemed present in a great overload, the following lines are naked and empty in contrast. Frost does manage to keep talking, but we could say "just barely." Another way to say this is to say that Frost comes on strong but then in the presence of "whispering," that little wisp of a word, has to get suddenly gentle and careful. The shift in tone, in approach, is marked. A steamshovel picks up a dime; a powerful drumroll brings out an actor with laryngitis; a rampaging elephant is made to stop to sniff a flower. In this sense, then, "whispering" is a big disappointment. Had the syntax allowed "whisper" would have been considerably stronger, taking the lead from "never" in line one. Never/ whisper has a hard imperative tone to it. But the extra syllable, the "ring" at the end, pulls our voice down and out; the word fizzles and fizzles out.

In the perfect poems of Robert Frost, the great poems, and "Mowing" I want to say is one, nothing is lost, everything is useful. Here in this poem turned to pledge the praise of work I want to say everything works. We can avoid the void, the low pressure area which follows in lines three and four and five and six simply by accepting that low pressure as a necessary and inevitable part of the work. Intensity, exertion, can't last forever—something Frost might have said. Or this is the calm after the storm, or the period where Frost regathers breath and wit to come at us again in full fury. But this is different too from just a period of rest and recuperation, for here too we hear the poet beginning on more of his famous "considerations." "What was it it whispered?" he asks, in the voice of the word itself. Another dimension is to see how Frost's sudden gentleness prepares the way, sets the precedent for, Frost's tender treatment of the flowers and snake later on. They too are fragile things, which offer small resistance to the scythe swung by one with Frost's grand purpose and design. And Frost might well have overloaded them in the larger plotting after meaning as he juggles fact and truth and love and dream in the further struggles yet to come.

The next three or four lines are not so interesting. There's nothing flashy going on, except we might well use this time and space more fully to appreciate the wonders we have witnessed. I think often I just get a little numb, having been overwhelmed, that I lose my place in the poem and don't come awake again until maybe line 7 for its employment of the negative again: "It was no dream of the gift of idle hours." The fact is that by line three and four we have made the transition to the interior of Frost's head and are involved with him in his investigation of reality. The sound of the scythe remains, perhaps as music for our contemplations, or as background, or that reminder which spurs us on. But whatever visual scene "beside the wood" provided is faded now. Physical reality is embodied in the whisper of consonants and in the recurring rising meter at line ends. To the extent Frost's relaxed nature in lines 3 through 6 provide the proper balancing to the highly concentrated movement in the first lines, a line like number 7 needs something rather substantial to jump out of. And so he creates the illusion of engagement, this time accomplished by the sheer bulk of language, the amassing the lines make simply by accumulating. Meanwhile his modesty and careful honesty are centermost, and we are reminded again that it is not Frost's conclusions we so depend on as the reasonable and thorough proceedings of his mind. Nonetheless, the middle of "Mowing" is not friendly territory for me. I am not one for daydreams, and I find it just as easy as Frost does to discredit easy gold and magic riches and fairy tales. What Frost pays attention to as he dismisses them are for me not serious alternatives, and I am not reluctant to let them go. "Or easy gold at the hand of fey or elf" has an old-fashioned sound to it, "poetic" in its image, archaic too, and rather sing-song in its meter. It is as if the scythe's monotony of movement has taken control of the mind's selection process. Much of the middle section of the poem stalls or evaporates—even Frost's modesty seems in excess, perhaps again an over-adjustment to his arrogant brilliance earlier. In line nine, however, things get rather lively again.

"Anything more than the truth would have seemed too weak": Frost is working again here; you can almost feel him straining his way through the line. "Anything," for starters, by reversing the iambic which has moved all the way into the beginnings of lines 6, 7, and 8, shows his resistance to the rhythms of the scythe. For this is a poem not only that goes along in accord with the powerful sound and brings it to life for us but which also analyzes the sound and asks that it speak in a voice we can comprehend, that it make sense. So far in the poem Frost has done a fine job showcasing the sound. The burden now is to assess its import. Maybe the burden began earlier even in line 2 in how it broke so strongly against the meter line 1 ended with. Right there Frost may have been saying, perhaps, among so many other things that it was hard to focus on, that one can't just go along, can't just go with the flow. That his resistance is felt through all those syllables that won't stay suppressed for anybody's iamb, even an iamb which is somehow the rhythm of life itself. Now in line 9 Frost may not have all those stressed syllables to begin with, but he works against the flow. Where there was an anapest and iamb we now have dactyls, two to start with—"anything more than the"—and then a heap of stressed syllables at line end—"truth would have seemed too weak." I think we very much feel the line length here, as much as we can also see it. Frost has been pushing the ten-syllable line toward twelve syllables throughout—many lines count to eleven. "Too weak" stands out a bit further perhaps because as we listen to line endings we just haven't had any which end on double stress. Line 9 gets long partly by starting with a stress, which we normally have to wait for (nearly all the lines start on less-stressed syllables) and then gets longer even more by running over—it is in fact the first enjambment of the poem. Any way it carries effort—it carries the search for the right words. It is as if Frost says "Wait a minute—this is not easy to say."—and then, rather falteringly, says it. Or begins to say it. It is a lot to say:

> Anything more than the truth would have seemed too weak
> To the earnest love that laid the swale in rows,
> Not without feeble-pointed spikes of flowers
> (Pale orchises), and scared a bright green snake.

The "earnest love" line is extremely regular in meter. We have heard its like before; the meter of line 1 is the same but for its extra syllable in the second syllable of "Never." The difference between the lines is seemingly slight, but in fact we have come a long ways between the expansive eloquence of line 1, grand enough to waste breath on the wind, and line 10 where Frost is so much in a nose-to-the-grindstone mood. The poet is earnest here, very precise, the anapest which leads off followed by four iambs demonstrates a careful measuring and refining of idea. Frost is moving in on his elusive quarry. Having started out from a vague "something," he has moved on to "dream" and "gift" and "gold" and "truth," naming each, feeling them out for their usefulness, abandoning each in turn. Now it is "love" whose measure he'll take. Is it love? Is love the answer? That the love is "earnest" makes a stronger case for it since Frost is extremely spare with adjectives in his best poems. He is a nouns and verbs poet, a fact and act poet. Gold in line 8 was "easy," but it was refused. And by denying the "easy gold" he has prepared us to embrace even more firmly its rhythmic equivalent in "earnest love." More importantly, Frost makes "earnest love" the force behind or within the scythe. It is the earnest love that "laid the swale in rows." Thinking, reasoning, rational man becomes somehow subordinate to the urgent earnest love that works here; the intellect that attempts to sort through possible meanings is carried along in the forceful rhythm of work which will not be made to stop to look at its justifications. In line 10 that rhythm Frost identified so much as the sound of the scythe comes back with a vengeance.

Did Frost wish to stop here? Love is the answer in "Hyla Brook." Though it takes him in that poem a whole other line beyond the sonnet to get to it. Or why, having found "earnest love," isn't Frost content with his effort? It's hard to say. Maybe he is nervous of ending a poem upon the high-sounding which so much began with inflation. Or maybe being a poet so much committed to the line and where the line seeks to go he must by contract ride out the line to its conclusion, which he does—"that laid the swale in rows," only to discover that his senses once overridden by daydream are again activated. Frost in his dream poems is a lot like a Jekyl-Hyde character shifting between loggy dreamy states and moments of keen outer alertness, and unable to control (seemingly) the turning points. So a line like 10 begins with Frost squeezing down on meaning in his interior laboratory only to find himself, before the line is over, standing in the swale of the open field. This inner/outer/outer/inner movement may be extremely sudden in Frost—it can be accomplished in a syllable or two, or as the eye blinks. When it is effective it is supremely beautiful. When it dominates a poem like "Birches" or "After Apple Picking" it seems on display and is slowed down to a slow-motion we can watch and study, or may seem thematic. In a poem like "Mowing" it is also present but is here a threat to the poem's comfortable resolution. Frost is wonderful when read at length (among the finest poems) for how he can be, at his best, so unprogrammatic. Something that he controls or isolates on in one poem and makes tame will run wild in another poem, having wonderfully escaped. So Frost's poems, taken serially in whatever random order you impose, present us continuing high adventure. They are occasions of intense local disturbance and emergency where things get askew or slip from consciousness and must be gotten back into the neat corral of the poem again.

Or once set in motion, once inertia's overcome, the scythe rhythm does not run out easily. Or once set in motion the scythe becomes a law unto itself. Often I'm sure we've been doing something which takes control of us. I drill right through the board I am drilling into the board below which is in fact my tabletop. Or pushing the lawn mower I am unable to avoid running over the dog bone left in the grass—I catch a glimpse of its round bald socket before the rotating blade hacks at it in fearsome noise and maybe to bend the shaft. The ambitions in Frost's poems are so often greater than we might preconceive, and grow as the poem goes along. It does not suit him merely to lay hold to some salient aspects of this reality, that the scythe has a sound which infects his talk, or that monotonous labor leads to a daydream where the poet can construct fantasies or search out meanings. Frost's loyalty is to wholeness, not only to climbing the birch trees but coming back down to earth at whatever risk is involved. Inflation or going up or ascending is no more risky or astonishing than coming down. "That would be good both going and coming back," he says in that poem. A similar need infects "Mowing." Or the inevitable is allowed to run its course, the scythe rhythm ridden out to exhaustion.

The love/scythe cuts and lays the swale in rows. Order from chaos. What a neat choice is "swale," late in a poem dominated by the brilliance of "whispering." It says perhaps that we are beginning to escape the force field of "whispering," or that we have escaped through time and distance, to set up our demanding process of analysis within the very consonance which keeps the mystery. "Swale" falls easily before the onslaught of "earnest love"—it goes down like straw in the unruly grasses which comprise it. It falls again before the rhythm of the scythe, the whole word struck as one downswing. Something about "swale" is unattractive. It sounds too much like "swine" or "swear" or "sweat" or "swamp" or "swill," and shares their unsavouriness. As measured against "earnest love" and the powerful drive of the scythe, "swale" is nature at its least noble or potent. The swales we have neglected or pushed through or paved over for parking lots of hamburger joints run from coast to coast, and as a people we are still finding them and subduing them. One man's orderly ecology full of wonder is always someone else's swale. And, as always, Frost, our hero, is of at least two minds. Attracted as he is to the ordering of chaos, turning the natural into the human, and doing the right work done generation by generation of keeping back the woods from the once-cleared ground, he builds too overwhelmingly a case for order. "Swale" is almost a dirty word, an unmentionable among the higher callings of "truth" and "dream" and "love." In Frost's incredibly agile mind, and in a poem which is founded upon overreaction and groundless assertions, Frost wakes from the sleepy dream of thought to discover how neat and snug he would make the world. Swale is a simplification, almost an affront to reality, and no fit word for the pale orchises and green snake. The swing of the scythe is wide and one learns to trust gravity to bring us back to our senses—just as in "Birches" gravity brings the boy back kicking to the ground. "Mowing," it may be said, introduces this metaphor, which is so central in much of Frost's best work.

Not without feeble-pointed spikes of flowers
(Pale orchises), and scared a bright green snake.

These are, by all accounts, the most rushed lines in the poem. They have a spell-shattering quality to them, a rushing-around-to make-oneself-presentable quality in the face of being accused of wasted time and idle thoughts. They make me wonder how close to being out of control of the sonnet Frost becomes, how ungainly this poem can seem. They also counterpose against Frost's growing intellection some unpleasant details, some hard facts that were almost smothered in the tossed grasses of the flurried work. Perhaps that's why they're rushed. Those forces which assert orderliness and interpretive action are taking control of the poem rather nicely. Scene and objects are getting left further and further behind. Frost has planted his feet on solid ground so that he may come into our hearts with singing, so that he can disclose, like some magician, the great truths bursting their buttons with anticipation.

Any poem is an act of definition, an exercise in just how conscious the poet will try to be, or how much consciousness the poet will try to account for. Frost's ambitions in "Mowing" have grown huge, perhaps too big for the rather studied and conventional format he imposes on himself. Strain is beginning to show—any poet who gets along for eleven lines without a parenthesis and maybe 500 lines afterwards without one is dangerously close to the breaking point. "Pale orchises" is a bulge on this otherwise trim poem—they set into the poem a wobble that threatens to throw the poem off center. Or is it that Frost has gone himself so far along with himself that it is only by some forceful wrenching that he can get these details into place.

Of course there is, at the same time, something fresh and wonderful about them. From having swung out too far to one extreme—of demeaning nature—Frost swings home to compensate the other way with all the tenderness he lavishes on the flowers. They are "feeble-pointed spikes," a curious phrase, combining images both of things enfeebled, ineffectual, limp, lifeless and also, contrarily, sharp and threatening. They are spikes in that they have been cut, and I think that whatever amount of threat they contain in "spikes" goes back to Frost's earlier attempt to discredit the swale of nature. If it is ugly we pay it no heed or we cut it with impunity, and if it is threatening besides, so much the better. But with the phrase "pale orchises" Frost gives us that wonderful reminder of the fragile beauty we were in danger of destroying without regret, and in parentheses that beauty is made even more delicate and precious. This is not some wasted sympathy Frost often attacks in the poetic-minded, but it does, by position here, very much hang precarious in the outcome. It is that true loveliness we almost lose access to in the act of defending ourselves and our claims. I began talking about "Mowing" by admiring Frost's boldness. Now, in a poem which is so close to being done, where Frost has his back to the wall, "pale orchises" is also bold. He who has been so busy trying to put a name to what the scythe whispered, now, nearly having accomplished that ambition, recants, draws back, <u>thinks twice</u>, and discovers that a name exists already for a thing of truth and dream and beauty and love— the flowers we call "orchises." They are not "easy gold," and not even a shade of gold, and have then little to do perhaps with profit or value, and "pale" as adjective is certainly not the match for old muscle-bound "earnest." They are that "tuft of flowers" the mower leaves for us in every poem to remind us that there is a limit to our knowing. "There are some things too big for the world," Richard Howard has Walt Whitman say, in respect to some other "harmless heliotrope," "that crowd it out at the sides." Howard must have been recalling that bulge Frost allowed on the otherwise round world of "Mowing."

Out of such precious but slightly uncomfortable facts as flowers and snakes, and earlier "the heat of the sun," Frost will build his fact, the large fact of line 13. By line 13 what came on us in an awkward rush and nearly tore the poem apart has been absorbed—in one of those compelling Frost-like consolidations he is famous for. It is one of the rules of a Frost poem that whatever accidents occur, whatever in yielding to pressures of circumstance the poem then comes to say, must blurt out like a witness on the stand under a rigorous cross examination—that all this will be taken in and reconciled against the growing larger purpose or some heretofore unexpected scale of ambition. Not elf or fey but flowers and snake. Not language which finds itself in endless juggling of abstractions, words made for explaining ourselves to ourselves, but language anchored in things, the things we love, or things we scare or scare us as they remind us we are too alone or not alone at all. Frost does, however, take some immediate advantage out of what at one time seemed about to make a mess of things. Lines 11 and 12 are awkward and force us to leap about and twist and turn askew to get them through. They are like a difficult moment in a figure-skating ballet where balance and plan are in jeopardy and it is only by some extraordinary power or grace that the skater survives. The performance may always thereafter seem flawed, but we have at the same time been given an index of difficulty, a sense of how close to disaster the skater skates. Frost is that skater here, who almost loses his balance. Or if there is still pressure on the poet, and I think there is, the pressure is displaced to line 13. What will he say? How will the poet account for that expanded consciousness which now includes sympathy for little things:

The fact is the sweetest dream that labor knows.

Line 13 is for some, perhaps, a disappointment. "Sweetest dream" is close to cliché while other things here seem so strange and unheard of as to be unassimilable. Frost often combines the overly recognizable (things we are fatigued by) with things so incredibly original we've never heard them before. Line 13 has an aphoristic quality many readers in Frost seek. It creates the illusion of meaning, of summing up. I would like to see it on a thousand sweatshirts, or stitched on a sampler for a wall.

Maybe by being vague enough it suggests a hundred uses. Or maybe something with a hundred uses has no one true real use at all. Frost would seek meaning in mystery he forces upon himself as the antidote for being complacent. The world has meaning, or it must. Or like a Don Quixote he goes on to tilt at windmills or at the delusions of his own having taken himself so seriously. If we transcribe this within the dynamic of the poem things become easier. Lines 11 and 12 create a turmoil which we work through tortuously, only to emerge that much more grateful for having emerged into a place of released turmoil, a clearing. Line 13 is that clearing, that seeming clarity in which things are properly named and explained. The reader, having bumped along, is cradled once again by an authoritative voice. It says that all is well. It sounds as if it says that all is well. And in its sounds it vanquishes the dull monotonous rhythm of the scythe, the rhythm of the scythe that made us cut the flowers down, that forced the dreaming on us at the start. We break from lines 11 and 12 into a more substantial place, having accounted for the cost of this labor, having realized the beauty we are unkind to, the snake so innocently bright and green despite our typical aversion. Line 13 is a kind of triumph, certainly the sort of thing we have been working toward. Not fantasy dream of idle hours, not things which are more than the truth, not "love" wearing enhancers like "earnest" to emphasize its seriousness, nor love carried in the rhythm of the scythe, where responsibility is displaced to something else.

But the line is finally a mystery. Finally the line is not sufficient. Finally it is not even the last line. Finally there is no finally. Or there is the world again. Imagine "Mowing" as a dialogue between things as they are or seem to be in themselves and meanings we want them to comply with. For all Frost's efforts toward formulations in lines 4 through 10 (and these are serious efforts, for the most part), the flowers and snake come back to lie at our feet to be reminders of the ground on which we walk. For all that line 13 stretches around to engulf and justify and absorb, the final line of the poem restores physical context, the small everyday facts of the scythe's sound in the real world if not to triumph over meaning then at least to balance with the large Fact of ultimate significance.

Frost's best poems do this kind of stretching. They oppose, sometimes more in earnest, sometimes more playfully, a natural it or essence against a poetry of insight or seeking. They oppose or they combine the natural and the human, taking advantage along the way of supposed or established distinctions between them (and thereby depending on the tensions they allow or encourage) while also creating the illusion that there is some solid middle ground between the two where things may be seen for what they are. The greatest poems are those of extreme restlessness, that which comes when accident or ambition leads the poem to embody a critical mass of consciousness where tension is at the breaking point. Where we will be glad for a resolution or what seems like one. Good as they are as poetry, and Frost has as fine an ear for language as anyone, and a disposition toward ambiguities that is also unmatched, the poems are as much about the ongoing unresolvable loveliness of the earth. So people talk so often of Frost's sweet sorrows, his wistfulness or waywardness. The danger is that we will go too far, or ask him to go too far, and ask for real finalities. Frost does not limit himself to real numbers; his poetry is the calculus of poetry where one is working toward infinities, toward finalities, but always toward. The only end we get to in "Mowing" is the period at the end of the last line.

Embracing the Guest at Last— Frost's Struggle in "My November Guest"

Reading "My November Guest" is a somewhat discouraging experience. The poem seems to have been steeped in tears. For those of us who admire Frost's vast resourcefulness and his brilliant wit, the poem bogs down in melancholy depiction of melancholy, the effect of which is only partially relieved in the final stanza. Things we get used to seeing Frost do right again and again, as if second nature, he either can't do at all here, or, having done them once, forgets in a line or two and reverts to more of the same old habits. The problem of course is that "My November Guest" is not one of Frost's triumphant later poems but a poem from his apprenticeship. It was published in *A Boy's Will*, the first book, a book from which we can take almost nothing now to illustrate the mature poet. "Mowing" remains the one masterpiece, "The Tuft of Flowers" offers some beautiful passages and an ambitious formal effort, and then there are the occasionally-gorgeous "October" and the technically-brilliant "Reluctance," but most of the poems are the work of nineteenth-century poetic diction and sympathies. Trying to teach some of the least of the poems once, "Now Close the Windows" and "Stars," I was startled to find them so obviously undone, incomplete, and, even, in the case of "Stars," grammatically incoherent. And yet the book remains exciting. In it we bear witness to first stirrings and the drama of the emergence of the young wayward poet into the first fulfillments of his power. On almost every page, amongst all so much that is embarrassing to us, there is some small showing of the greatness to come. Here and there among lines that could have been written by anyone of Frost's generation there are lines that can only have been written by Robert Frost. Reading the book as a whole, or reading transitional poems like "October" among the others, is like panning for gold or hunting antiques in a used furniture barn. One always feels that something important may happen at any moment. This excitement is compounded in the fact that *A Boy's Will* was published by a man already old enough to be the father of that boy, and so while many poems are immature in technique they are old and wise in emotion, and so we get a poignant blend of exuberance and world-weariness, which turns out to be so much the psychological composition of Robert Frost the man.

The early poems are full of awkward longings but profound passion too. And there is a rawness to them Frost valued and which he worked hard to keep.

"My November Guest" is clearly then a hybrid, old and new ways, language already tired of being poetry mixed with language that has not been poetry before. It is a pretty poem to hear, to read aloud, perhaps because it is so lugubrious. My challenge will be to try to say what makes the poem more than pretty, what makes it more than a curiosity. I am not sure I can do this, however, without resorting to something rather mechanical first, the sorting out of what still seems fresh and vigorous from what seems old-fashioned, poetic, and stale. Such sorting is a personal matter. I will reject something you would not. But what is more important than any agreement is the process of investigation which will open the poem gently to scrutiny. At various times, in trying to do this sorting, I have made two columns for myself, a sort of debits/credits ledger. I'd like to make a quick listing here.

The season is dark, and so Frost's mood is dark. This is a problem. The poet appears no more autonomous than a barometer. He seems incapable of independent thought or action. He embodies weather, is the verbal equivalent of a "sodden pasture." There is an amazing passivity to the poet. He is a grand receiver—he does not initiate. The mind, for Frost, is like a sponge. In the presence of rain it absorbs rain. It doesn't have the power to resist, to shed it or shake it off. No waterproofing. In the more-mature poems the poet is emotionally and spiritually self-governing. He has his own reservoir of dispositions. He develops a skin, a hide, to prevent untoward absorption of atmospheres. He develops a self-regulating, self-stabilizing intelligence. This development may even become a source of pride for the poet. In the great tiny poem "One Step Backward Taken" Frost flaunts the accomplishing of his incredibly useful reserve:

> Not only sands and gravels
> Were once more on their travels,
> But gulping muddy gallons
> Great boulders off their balance

Bumped heads together dully
And started down the gully.
Whole capes caked off in slices.
I felt my standpoint shaken
In the universal crisis.
But with one step backward taken
I saved myself from going.
A world torn loose went by me.
Then the rain stopped and the blowing
And the sun came out to dry me.

Frost's strategic retreat here would be almost indecently smug were it not for the suicidal infection he attributes to everything around him. But in the *Boy's Will* poems Frost is immobilized. And yet the intense sensitivity he shows is just that responsiveness and openness to the world that we expect of major poetry.

The vocabulary is a vocabulary of the pretty and the poetic. This too is a problem. Or it is the same problem as above examined for its manifestations in diction. Almost invariably the poems of *A Boy's Will* are poems of the adjective and the adverb. They have about them a decorative quality. Their language is distractedly pretty, superficial, as if the emotional component of the poem is like an applied lacquer—surface only, and does not go deep, does not penetrate muscle or bone. In "One Step Backward Taken," in contrast, Frost is extremely physical. He steps aside, away from, his whole body moves. Had "One Step" been attempted in the mode of "My November Guest" instead of stepping the poet might have wept, or blanched. We would have had to visit him in the recovery room. The later better poems are full of nouns and verbs. They do the work, and the poems are about work, the work thought is. A poem like "Mowing," for example, attracts us for how rich it is in concrete physical detail not merely beheld but experienced. The earlier weaker Frost does not engage the world through his body. He is lazy. He looks and leaves. Or he tries to do everything with his mind alone. The poem is then that thing made to substitute for action, and as such it is defensive about its inactivity. Passivity becomes aggressive. It looks for excuses as to why it wasn't on time, why it gave up, why it was in a bad mood. It barricades itself behind the adjective. It smothers its nouns. Its days are dark, its tree is withered, its mist is clinging, earth faded, sky heavy. Its adjectives cling to its nouns in a suffocating embrace, making them heavy and us sleepy. Clusters of adjectives surround a noun like the body's defense system around the invader, something foreign to itself, something from outside the self. A huge struggle ensues. But the only sign of this struggle is a slightly-elevated temperature and a flushed cheek. The poet lies on the couch, all day, exhausted.

Some of Frost's language is clearly not enough his own. "Beautiful," used twice in "My November Guest," is a "poetry kit" word, what every apprentice poet gets when he sends away for the guaranteed money-back offer. By 1922 the word has all but disappeared from Frost's vocabulary. Other phrases and expressions are even more obviously poetic, even more obviously archaic. "Fain to list" is probably the worst example, where "list" is listen, abbreviated to fit the meter and rhyme. "Vexes" is a verb, and so draws real energy from that, but is unrelievedly old-fashioned. Even "let me stay" doesn't mean what it says but is a substitute for "will not let me be at ease with myself" or something like this. There is padding too, words put in to prop the meter or fill out the line. "Truly" in line 13 is one of them, perhaps the most glaring one. "Simple" in line 9 may be another. These are wasted words. They make the poem numb, or more numb than it has to be.

> My Sorrow, when she's here with me,
>   Thinks these dark days of autumn rain
> Are beautiful as days can be;
> She loves the bare, the withered tree;
>   She walks the sodden pasture lane.
>
> Her pleasure will not let me stay.
>   She talks and I am fain to list:
> She's glad the birds are gone away,
> She's glad her simple worsted gray
>   Is silver now with clinging mist.

The desolate, deserted trees,
  The faded earth, the heavy sky,
The beauties she so truly sees,
She thinks I have no eye for these,
  And vexes me for reason why.

Not yesterday I learned to know
  The love of bare November days
Before the coming of the snow,
But it were vain to tell her so.
  And they are better for her praise.

This is a poetry of the line, not the sentence. Frost begins, like many of his generation, as a poet of the line, but he becomes, triumphantly, a poet of the sentence. The poet of the line is concerned with similarities, not differences. He is essentially conservative and cautious—he will not venture very far that he does not get anxious and return to where he used to be. The poet of the line is patiently relentlessly parallel. He lays it on in layers. He has a high tolerance for the static, or if he permits change or movement it is over tiny barely-perceptible increments. He is not a maker of new things so much as a duplicator of old. He stamps out molds in which to pour his words. He measures lengths, fills in the gaps and chinks. Having learned what the rules are, the poet of the line makes a virtue of obedience. When he arrives, breathless, tired, at the end of the line, or maybe not tired at all, still he pauses or he stops. He does not wish to appear impetuous. And so meter dominates the poetry of the line:

Her pleasure will not let me stay.
  She talks and I am fain to list:
She's glad the birds are gone away,
She's glad her simple worsted gray
  Is silver now with clinging mist.

This is meter stiff and strict and metronomic. Hearing a few lines of it we are taken hold by a drug and made dopey.

Under its influence, we walk as if asleep, with short regular steps. Our feet are heavy. Under its influence the poet is likely to say anything, just so long as it complies with the form, but it is just as likely he will say nothing at all. End stop punctuation dams up the thought, keeps it from going "too far," insists upon parallel development rather than the more-reckless and surprising linear variety. Of the first fifteen lines of "My November Guest" only two are enjambed, all the rest are screwed down tight with heavy ornate hardware. And what an assortment of hardware it is. Fifteen little lines but four periods, six commas, one colon (where it doesn't make sense anyway), and two semicolons (in consecutive lines). So shades of the prison house close about the free spirit, so language parades its chains. Monotony of meter begs relief in rhyme, but end stop punctuation forces too much emphasis upon the rhyme, and rhyme responds by becoming both loud and inelastic. Scrutiny at line ends reinforced through meter and the strict maintenance of syllable count keeps the rhymes pure to the extent they become overly predictable, common and unimaginative. Strict meter also abstracts meanings. By breaking words at the syllable turns within a strong format the integrity of polysyllabic words is compromised. "Beautiful," not a vivid word in any case, becomes "beáu/tǐ/fúl," and loses some of what little identity it has. Poetry of the line subordinates phrasal autonomy as well to a strict recurring pattern. "Simple worsted gray," scattered along the meter, puts "simple" in a slack and indefinite relationship to what follows instead of how it should be. By emphasizing stressed syllables one would expect that certain words, one-syllable words especially, and if they are nouns and verbs, would gain emphasis and become memorable. But because everything is on the same level, or is being raised to the same level, we end up with a collection of elements all treated equally and nearly interchangeable. Who can remember the dominant words of "My November Guest"? Are there <u>birds</u> in the poem? Leaves? Stones? Rain? Also because meter is so inelastic when polysyllabic words are broken in stress these stressed units compete for attention with monosyllabic stressed words. We have then not only birds, days, bare, lane, fain, glad, eye, but also "tru," "beau," "simp," "sert," "vem," and others. Stressed syllables of all sorts clog and clot, or make a clutter. We come away with no sure sense of what has transpired except that we have witnessed a quantification. Similarly, stanzas take precedence over the natural flow of the thought. Some of the great appeal of "The Road Not Taken" is precisely that it overflows its boundaries, that it is expressive of urgency in that it allows the sentence to keep making its way not only through line ends without stopping but over the intervals of stanzas as well. The two poems are definitely worth contrasting. Both are twenty lines long, both use the abaab-rhyme pattern, both are four five-line stanzas. But where "The Road Not Taken" is characterized by continual surprises, and ends up not at all where one expects it to end, indeed is one of Frost's most strange and wonderful poems, "My November Guest" seems repetitive, dull, tired, and both overwritten and underwritten at the same time. In pure mechanical format the two poems are nearly look-alikes, and to the extent that form continues to seek out the terms of its fulfillment "My November Guest" may be the prototype for "The Road Not Taken." But form in the earlier poem tyrannizes Frost, uses and abuses him, whereas in "The Road Not Taken" form and content are in a more happy equilibrium.

We need to talk too about Frost's figure of Sorrow, his personifying the emotion, making it a woman and a guest in his home. This is a quaint approach, certainly, and more than suspect for us who worry about the implicit sexism of language. A poet like Robert Bly, who harangues us on behalf of bringing the masculine and feminine together within each of us, would see the way this poem finally turns as a rather exciting union of the two, even though the poem is pointed more importantly toward other matters, and irregardless of whether Frost is an especially good example of "the divided self." Such matters cannot be resolved here, nor are such matters usually raised by the average reader reading the poem. Stylistic concerns are much more pressing, and stylistically what Frost does is singularly quaint. The contemporary reader will probably find the maneuver embarrassing in its labored indirection, almost cute. For those of us raised on Robert Lowell and Sylvia Plath, two poets who come to mind prominently as our poets of "sorrow," Frost's elaborate indirection may seem to result from lack of nerve. But restraint is not necessarily cowardice. Interestingly, what the fierce and forthright encounters of Plath and Lowell lack is just some such normalizing reserve, some essential dignity of politeness. Such great lengths they go to strip themselves naked before us, to raise their desperate honesty to heroic levels, I for one begin to wish for a little more modesty, a little stronger sense of what is proper in disclosure and confession. Frost's power over us now, post-Lowell, post-Plath, and in spite of all the baring and unnerving of Sexton and Berryman, may be just this, that he retains some essential civilizing reserve. It is the old Kurtz/ Marlowe conflict. We have had all these Kurtzes—men and women who looked into the abyss and got dizzy and fell, or who themselves were hell, and are lost to us. Frost is our Marlowe among the poets. He seeks to mediate the horror, to spread it, to divide it, to find form in which to confine it, and design through which to explore it.

But if the feminine Sorrow cannot help but seem old-fashioned to us, then such a quality need not be to the poem's detriment. Much is made of how our scholars tend to be conservative, and niggardly in rewarding laurels to poets until years after their deaths. But it may take decades to fully appreciate a writer's qualities. What he or she does, how he or she sounds, must be sorted out from everything else it resembles and sounds like, and we must, perhaps, lose interest in whatever hopes and fears the events of that time would normally inspire in us. In other words, the poet must seem to become a tragic figure, whose power to change others and change himself not only is limited but may have ceased altogether if the poet has died. I expect, therefore, a new and especially useful Frost criticism now, within the next ten years. Nearly all of what we've had on Frost so far was written while he was alive, and nearly always by friends of the poet, or his enemies or rivals. Some more-recent work has been done by students of Frost's or people who could have been his children. As those of vested interest give up their claims other special interests will of course take over, but this present period seems conducive to studies that are more objective.

Greg Kuzma

Given the time of composition for "My November Guest" the quaintness I speak of may well have been a problem Frost himself was aware of, perhaps subliminally. "My November Guest" is a transitional poem, and so we find in it, among much that is given and beyond the poet's conscious control, the emergence of control itself. Melodramatic as the personification of Sorrow is, Frost exploits it brilliantly in his final stanza. Even with all its disadvantages the split of the self into the oversensitive Sorrow and some different self creates a wonderful tension. Because Sorrow is identified with the excessively romantic poet of moods, poet as victim of feelings, Frost's other self, who finally responds in the last stanza, may be said to transcend the former self. From such perspective "My November Guest" becomes a benchmark, a breakthrough poem, a milestone. Given a definition of poetic progress which is not cooperative but which cares only for the time being, only for one fallible and imperfect poem and what may there be realized, such a breakthrough as here may not overturn the existing order and may even be forgotten by the poet later on. So Frost can write "My November Guest," achieve briefly its ecstatic awareness, and then fall back into old habits or find other new bad ones. Which is probably what happens. Yet this poem is certainly one that had to have been written in order that Frost be able to write "The Oven Bird," for instance. The identification of poet with the speaking bird is a variation upon what Frost does here.

What does Frost achieve in dividing himself? As I've said already he creates the preconditions for conflict, competition, rivalry, all of which lends tension to the poem. If the tension is not perceived at once, and is not really present in the opening stanzas, and is only fully expressed when Frost's second self replies in stanza four, the poem may be said only to have been temporarily misleading. Or it gains in drama with the suddenness and the surprise with which the conflict is joined. Having postponed the conflict, and hiding any hints of it until then, is certainly a bold and risky maneuver. The first three stanzas are so saturated by the sodden emotionality of Sorrow that many readers may dismiss the poem or stop reading before finishing it. But the procedure bears a commensurate yield of power. There is, suddenly, along with the possibility for conflict, the possibility of dialogue, interaction, cooperation and communion. Perhaps forgiveness. These more positive dimensions are maybe less compelling for us than conflict and confrontation. On the current scene our great poet of harmony, Wendell Berry, is perceived by many not to be a poet at all. Because he feels too good he cannot be serious. If communion and harmony are to be aesthetically effective there must be as conscientious a presentation of disharmony. Berry's poems often leave the disharmony implied, or prior to the scene of the poem, or to an understanding readers already familiar with his work may have made. Frost too often has this problem. He has it in most of the other early poems from *A Boy's Will*, notably in "A Prayer in Spring," a poem often used as an example of Frost's true voice, but which should never be. And he has it again in his later work where Frost's fears and griefs are drugged into oblivion by the narcotics of praise and success. The speaker in most of Frost's poems after 1925 is immensely more secure and immensely more self-satisfied, and often speaks the entire poem in the mode of he who has triumphed. And so the great poems of loss and the struggle against loss become fewer and fewer.

Frost's division of himself works to another advantage. It creates within the poem a set of conditions or events which may then be analyzed. Such a procedure is most typically Frost's where the poems so often begin with exposition or notation and end in analysis and interpretation. It is the procedure of the scientist too, the specimen hunter who allows as much room as necessary for the acquisition of things or the accumulation of data. One must always be careful not to be too sloppy about it, not to pollute the specimen, and to be extremely generous in allowing nature or whatever it is to be itself, to be natural. Few have talked about the influence of science or psychology upon Frost's work—or if they do it is to show Frost as resistant to and antagonistic to science. In "My November Guest" however, he gives over almost the entire session to the morbid infatuations of Sorrow. Something similar is going on in "Mowing." There the scythe is a powerful force. Combined in and through the body it makes a strong impression on us that it has something to tell us, something it knows that we might well listen to. No two of Frost's great poems are ever fully alike—that's partly why they are each so effective—Frost in the writing of them works as someone who knows he is into something heretofore undiscovered or undeveloped. A room opens, previously hidden, or a new music begins to sound. In "Mowing" Frost is quick to intervene with questions and theories, in "My November Guest" he acts as if he never will.

Another advantage of Frost's division of himself into two selves is that thereby he makes himself larger. When I was talking earlier about the poetry-kit poeticisms and conventions that were handed down to him, Frost's acceptance of those and reuse of them was the act of someone willing to be confined by their limits, or unable to escape those limits. The self of many of those early poems is a small and narrow self, a young and immature poet. But now, in "My November Guest," the poet has grown a second self, one that is potentially greater and not just different from the earlier self. What the relationship between the two selves will be is of course what makes the final stanza so exciting. After the long reiteration of gloom in the first fifteen lines, Frost's second self might well be nothing more than his own exhaustion or boredom. The growing larger, and the awareness of that growth which seems suddenly to burst upon the poet, is an extremely compelling situation to witness. Frost does not yet contain multitudes, but he has made a quantum leap into a larger awareness.

What I have been trying to do is mix talk of Frost's procedure in the poem as regards to meaning and the opportunities derived thereby with comments I made earlier regarding the limitations Frost finds in nineteenth-century prosody. I want to assert that Frost's impatience with the voice of Sorrow in the poem and his beautifully balanced response to that voice in his last stanza is also a metaphor for Frost's technical impatience with the language he inherited and whose constraints he was restless to escape. "My November Guest" becomes then a declaration of independence—the look and feel of the new freedom can be experienced in and through the prosody. Where earlier lines began by dutifully cranking up their iambic meter, Frost breaks out in the first syllable of the final stanza with the strongly-stressed "Not." He will *not* hold his tongue a moment longer.

> Not yesterday I learned to know
> The love of bare November days
> Before the coming of the snow,
> But it were vain to tell her so,
> And they are better for her praise.

Earlier, in stanza one, we did have some substitution into the basic iambic regularity. Someone scavenging in "A Boy's Will" for evidence of the more mature Frost will be quick to snap up line two: "Thinks these dark days of autumn rain." Such an outburst, however, leads nowhere in the ensuing lines, and might be seen, in a poet who developed differently or not at all, to be no more than an aberration or even perhaps evidence of metrical clumsiness. "Not" is a surprise, a shock. And what follows, though in keeping with the iambic meter, is swift and strong speech, rapid and full of energy. Where Sorrow's voice is freighted down under the weight of everything it tries to speak about, and barely moves, at times, and stalls and sighs at commas and other pauses, the different speaker of the final stanza is bold and forthright and energetic. The change, though still in and of words, approaches the physical. When Frost reads the poem aloud his voice increases in volume, and deepens in pitch. One gets the inescapable impression that he is not reading the line this way by choice, or because his audience was getting restless, but by necessity, because it is *in* the words. If line can be made to show it, then we will note that these lines of stanza four do not stall and stop and glance about helplessly at their ends—they plunge on carried along beyond their imposed limit by the force of statement and by some greater urgency than can be properly partitioned off and measured. Frost's other self, bursting to be free, runs a long way before we get that comma, finally, at the end of line 3. And it is a comma, not a semicolon, not a colon, not a period. His speaker has more to say, more directly contingent upon these matters. The diction also throughout is manifestly physical, fully verbal. In three lines all the important words are verbs and nouns. Only "bare" stands in for all those smothery adjectives of Sorrow's speech. So Frost breaks out of the suffocating hold of the old ways.

Frost's breakout is many things at once. He is the fighter, beaten down successively round after round, who seems always on the verge of collapse, who suddenly revives at the very last second, to strike real blows for all the cheering crowd. This turnabout in the affairs of the speaker may have taught Frost something about the need for putting himself or some part of himself in jeopardy, and then, from that infirmity or diminishment, saving himself at the last moment. It is what he does in many of the great poems, from "One Step Backward Taken"—which is, really, a simplified metaphoric scheme for the procedure generally—all the way to "Desert Places" and "Directive." It is the retreat from the poetry of atmospheres too, and so bears directly on the lesson of "Hyla Brook" and its strange passage about "brooks taken otherwhere in song"—which makes a criticism of poets who are helplessly at the mercy of conditions as they find them. As well the turn of the final stanza reveals self-mastery—not just a refusal to do what others do, but to exert control over the less pleasant tendencies of the self. Making the self large—large enough so as to contain contradictions, large enough to serve then as a serious battleground—is essential for Frost's continued growth as a poet. That we believe him when he tells us things, that we accept his authority when he speaks, that we are convinced that his study has been thorough in even the shortest of poems, done the full job, owes itself to advances made in "My November Guest." The turn the poem takes is also an early example of where Frost, through understatement, is able to convince us that he has indeed suffered. This is a major problem for Frost critics, both those who don't like him or don't trust him and those who find him, as Trilling called him, a poet of terror. What we have here in this poem is not terror, by any means, but it is that loneliness and aloneness we all know or come to know be it from loss of season or loss of human harmony or affection. Interestingly, Sorrow's problem is not just that she feels so much, but that she enjoys it too much. Because Sorrow and Frost's second speaker are one and the same person, ultimately, the sentimental self-indulgent overstatement and the darker more-restrained stoic understatement, instead of canceling each other out, instead multiply effects. If it is true Frost stereotypes women here, the problem is not resolved in the poem but persists frighteningly into the male/female conflict of a poem like "Home Burial." This is merely November we're mourning here, gratefully, but even so Frost makes of it a wonderfully complex and rich poem.

"Vain" is a wonderful word in the second to the last line. It means both "vain" of him to speak to her, to presume upon Sorrow's suffering, that she would deign to hear him, that anyone's suffering can in any sense correct anyone else's, and it is also a short form of "in vain," meaning it would do no good. The play Frost makes does not stop here, however. Not only is it in vain for him to interrupt or interfere, but these days of suffering and sorrow are better for what Sorrow makes of them. This is a wise position, deriving as it must from prior sad experience enough in the ways of the world. It is a generous one too. Frost is behaving toward his "guest" as one should behave toward guests. We give them their space, we honor their concerns, we let them talk. They may not know how much we know full well what they profess to be so particularly injured by. But, Robert Frost says, we might do well to keep silent. Not that by doing so we show that we don't feel, don't think, not that we thereby deny our own pain and suffering, but that the slightest barest gesture is enough to express it. Reading the poem aloud Frost raises his voice, a little. And that is all. So anyone who studies Frost's work at length will discover how subtle it is, how much may be accomplished in the smallest gesture, and so the poem stands too as a standard for behavior, not just a way of carrying the self in poems carefully bound and ordered and restrained, but a way of carrying the self forth against the sorrows of the world at large. Reading "My November Guest," especially when we notice at the last that the second speaker does not in fact speak at all, makes of this an unforgettable lesson.

WHAT "THE ROAD NOT TAKEN" REALLY REALLY MEANS, REALLY

The Road Not Taken

Two roads diverged in a yellow wood,
And sorry I could not travel both
And be one traveler, long I stood
And looked down one as far as I could
To where it bent in the undergrowth;

Then took the other, as just as fair,
And having perhaps the better claim,
Because it was grassy and wanted wear;
Though as for that the passing there
Had worn them really about the same,

And both that morning equally lay
In leaves no step had trodden black.
Oh, I kept the first for another day!
Yet knowing how way leads on to way,
I doubted if I should ever come back.

I shall be telling this with a sigh
Somewhere ages and ages hence:
Two roads diverged in a wood, and I—
I took the one less traveled by,
And that has made all the difference.

One problem with "The Road Not Taken" is how insecure it seems when one pressures it for its conventional meaning. For decades, it seems, and in a thousand places, "The Road Not Taken" has been made to stand for being yourself, being an individual, avoiding the easier and more-travelled path, declaring one's own declaration of independence. Somehow in it must reside a real choice between divergent things. It is a poem teachers have taught students by, thereby investing them with the high ideals great literature always calls us to. Such an assortment of interpretations have gathered around the poem that the real poem, if there ever was one, and if we can ever get to it, may seem irrelevant. If poems were people what we have here is a movie star image entirely— something foisted upon the person underneath the image and upon us too against all our wills. Poems like people can get absorbed by a society's need to promote certain myths, to force whatever might in fact be truly unique or individual to comply with its collective identity. And a society like ours, which has little use for poetry except the decorative or the momentarily inspirational, will treat its poems and poets as badly as it treats its actors and sports heroes. What can be said of the poem is even more true of the poet: Frost has something important to tell us; he got old and he got gray and he got wise, and the poems are where his lessons are.

Frost himself is much to blame for the conventional view of the poem in that he allowed himself to read it so often without correcting for how he knew it was being misread. Or we can blame Frost for never setting the record straight anywhere regarding his poems. But what poet ever risked such a mission. To the extent a poet writes for readers or publication or speaks toward communication he necessarily admits to the imperfections of the process. You may speak as you will, that is how freedom allows it, we say, and we may hear you as we choose to, and understand you to our own purposes. (One could thereby argue that the conventional view of the poem is grounded in the very freedom inherent in creative writing and reading.) But ideas concerning freedom and the individual do not belong just to America, which would be big enough as measured against the play in any poem, but to humanity itself. To go one's own way, to be, even if briefly, different or unique. Such is the necessary conviction to all who strain to live among the hundred millions of our kind. Seen in this larger context Frost seems small and helpless and his ambitions but minimal equipment for living—how do we fault a poet for the little truths he would affect to hold to live.

I do not think there is any totally acceptable way to disentangle this poem from the conventional view. The view not only has persisted in the world so long but it perhaps is also a real component of the poem—a dimension of the context in which this poem or any poem is written. It may also have been an unconscious influence on Frost as he wrote. The speaker here *looks for* difference, as if he were programmed to do so. An interesting reading proposes that the speaker here is one of those people brought up on self-reliant individualism, someone from a classroom study of say "The Road Not Taken," and who attempts to put its precepts into practice. It is as if Robert Frost anticipates the misreading of the poem and tries to work through it or around it. And so we get what at times seems the laboratory tone—the cool scrutinizing coupled with careful and measured processing of material. At times the lines seem to be lines in a step by step procedure and the poet working his way through an ordered sequence.

And yet any careful reading of this poem must invalidate the conventional view. Frost's speaker may or may not be aware of this myth or that myth, but all his efforts to disprove the likeness of the two roads fails. They are equal: "And both that morning equally lay." It is only in the future that they are made different in hindsight. If not then the conventional view, what? Well, there is the fun of playing off hindsight and foresight. Foresight fails. But one might question also whether hindsight affords a proper understanding or vantage point. Or to go back earlier in the poem, to the first stanza, we can luxuriate in the time of deliberation:

> long I stood
> And looked down one as far as I could
> To where it bent in the undergrowth;

Measuring this episode against the poem as a whole, but twenty lines overall, we might conclude that Frost is enjoying this safe period before a choice is forced upon him, just as too we need to note the impulsive quality to the leap from the first road to the second across the gap between stanzas.

> Then took the other, as just as fair,
> And having perhaps the better claim,
> Because it was grassy and wanted wear;

Hindsight refers to what Frost rationalizes in his final stanza, but it might be appropriate to use the word here where the act of choosing precedes the justification for it. Poems proceed in time—they are made in time to tell time, to keep time, as Frost so well does here in meter and elsewhere. One thing necessarily precedes another, one thing follows another, and even as any poem's ultimate purpose may be to vanquish time or set forth in language what seems real and eternal against our own vanishing, poems fall victim to time as any reader of most of our poetry comes to realize. The thing then is to make so well against time, to know so well the forces arrayed against poetry and ourselves that we build well against these erosions. Frost's great aim was, he said, to place a few poems where they would be hard to get rid of. He has. TRNT is such a poem. And perhaps one of its secrets is in how thoroughly Frost has played with time (and maybe played *for* time as well) in this poem. The poem endures because it keeps step with time itself, because it is about our mind's measuring the world against the passage of time even as poetry it keeps time in meter and rhyme.

I sometimes feel that Frost is stalling, though I am glad he does, when he goes through all these little investigations of his:

> And sorry I could not travel both
> And be one traveler long I stood
> And looked down one as far as I could
> To where it bent in the undergrowth;

Then took the other, as just as fair,
And having perhaps the better claim,
Because it was grassy and wanted wear;
Though as for that the passing there
Had worn them really about the same,

And both that morning equally lay

This is a kind of walking talk, a talk in which we feel the motion, a talk which moves, as water does, but keeps its surface, a talk which moves like the stream of water or the stream of time. It is a lot of saying little, in any case, but only if we do not feel the urgency of the situation. Were Frost's speaker here a hero struggling to untie himself before the moving wall crushed him every syllable would be fraught with tension. It is the absence of any real pressure to the circumstance which makes the poem seem leisurely and speculative—which makes it feel like *poetry*.

Various issues surface here. I can side with that complaint that Frost does not provide us with context enough. His traveler might be out for an idle walk—or to pick flowers or look for leaves fallen in the road. Lawrence Thompson helps solve the puzzle by giving us the Edward Thomas story of how TRNT was written to show to Frost's nature walk companion one of Thomas's humorous traits—that whichever path or road was taken he wished they had gone some other way or the other way. This is a compelling story, and its satisfactions are many. It helps place the poem in circumstances, and helps give it an audience not ourselves so that we can feel embarrassed for having so long taken "everything said as personal to ourselves." Also it gives Frost's traveler a purpose, which he seems not to have been given, while also undermining the poem as statement of universal wisdom. Thompson goes on to say how Thomas didn't "get it," did not understand from the poem sent him by Frost that it was a joke on himself. I sympathize. Having the story makes the poem seem even more mysterious and perverse. By what strange process are we to understand Frost's work if his friends and companions who share his experiences cannot understand it.

Which is to say, perhaps, that we are as good readers of the finished poem, having only what we know to guide us. Or, the closer to the poet not necessarily the closer to the poem—that no one close to Frost understood him as he understood himself. Or the damage done to these people by time and by Frost deprived them of that free-floating objectivity that only the casual reader years later can bring to a poem. Who, in fact, was Frost writing *for*? Well, I think he was writing for poetry, on behalf of poetry, the angels.

Such a commitment exempts him from blame, from human failure or betrayal. But I do not want to take up here the discouraging weight of Frost's selfishness in his personal life as expressed not only by Thompson but by the poet's own poems and even by his voice in tape recordings. It's clear to anyone, I think, that here is a person totally absorbed in his own private conception of reality. If that conception betrayed love, if it permitted suicide and insanity among his children, we may weep for them and Frost too, but who can say, when absorbed by this most self-absorbed of poets, that any price was too high for art of this transcendent power.

Knowing about Frost's life and worrying about it is not an idle practice or beside the point. The poems themselves reach out to engage a universe in which little is known or secure. A poem like TRNT presents a kind of nakedness or passivity in a narrator with whom we must sympathize if we are ever at a loss in our own realities. By a lovely irony the incredible beauty of TRNT, the heartfelt ache of it, turns us back toward our own lives to making answers that may not have questions, the small things which let us live. I do not think of my own son when I read TRNT except that he has a journey too to make, to suffer and know, and I weep too for Frost's son Carol for what he lived and suffered, and for Frost whose great gift made so much else seem small and of little consequence.

Frost's poems encourage us toward tangents, encourage us to move out sideways in order to keep going on. But we must come back, and the question of context continues to remain. What is he out there for? What is this person doing? Is he out for leaves in the same way he is out for stars in another poem? Is he someone like ourselves in the midst of life, in the midst of life in which anything can happen, in which the seemingly insignificant can overwhelm us or lead us into getting lost and never finding out where we are or were or getting back. Traditionally this problem is solved by having the speaker be the "known" quantity of Robert Frost himself. It is Frost who tells us or someone with authority, a poet. And if we are squeamish of laying the poem to that authority, distrusting images, or distrusting autobiography, or hating Frost, or distrusting Thompson (as William Pritchard does in his new biography), we have the poem itself. But then there are those who distrust poetry. And so we can go another step and hate poetry, or another and distrust whatever we are told by others, and so trust only our own experience, ourselves along with whatever we can find ourselves. Stretching as far as this we may eventually arrive at a definition of a lean, unencumbered person, stripped naked in the universe, without illusions, who has only a few things he's gotten from experience, who does not throw himself forward on false pretenses or assumptions, or who does not judge hastily and who does not give himself over to easy conclusions. Curiously such a naked self is the speaker in TRNT.

This rounding out and back on itself, to come to oneself again, is one of the furious delights of this poem. And this process of getting Frost into the poem with all that we know of him, and then to discredit those associations in an effort to get him out, only to get back to the poem again, is precisely that process by which we come back to basic things, by which we discover how mind and matter are entangled. One thing I'm sure of, we do not ever rid ourselves of poems like TRNT unless we have ceased to care how we know or care about ourselves or the world.

Frost's skills as a poet, what he does and what he can't help but do are abundantly in evidence. Those who want to forget about Frost the man are everywhere reminded of Frost the poet. If this is a man with limits, this is a poetry with limits. This is a man who like ourselves knows certain physical realities— that we can't "travel" two roads at once "and be one traveler." A poet can't play tennis with the net up and also play with the net down. Or, finally, we can't get out of ourselves to be outside ourselves and still be ourselves. Physics tells us. That we look is a dimension of what we see—or taken further—we are what we know. So Frost's commitment to form is itself a reality. One paper spoils the other, Jake Barnes says. Reading the paper is itself a reality and is different from someone else reading the paper. Or James Dickey's famous black leopard in a zoo, hiding its spots in its black hide, reminds us of our limits: "Your moves are exactly right for a few things in this world." My reading of Robert Frost's "The Road Not Taken" is what it is, my reading.

Frost's "moves" are in fact exactly right for a few things in this world. I find myself comforted in interesting ways by his formal commitments. Many readers are. It's nice to observe such courtesies, even as they are perhaps archaic courtesies-- nostalgia is a profound feeling. We hold the past to us, and make it alive in the present. Much of the appeal Frost has for millions of readers may indeed be how he manages to be a poet of certainties. Readers also like to keep, as critics do, as poets reading other poets do, the nice distinction between themselves and "the other." Right now for us that distinction is partly the function of Frost's trusting form. We are in our conventions somehow wiser than Frost, or we will let him charm us for a while because he is safely a rhymer, and because he is safely dead. Part of my own rationalization in studying Frost is that basically he is a poet whose necessities cannot be mine; he does what I can't do, was not trained to do by the poets who brought me up—and do not want to do. Furthermore he represents a poetry which is actually popular, and so therefore discredited here amongst those of us who are so very sure to be great is to be misunderstood. Or we will point to Rod McKuen's popularity as one indicator of what the public deems to be poetry.

Things go fine here because Frost makes them go. We partake of this ritual because we are able to distance ourselves from it—we can come forward to the poem willingly. We can disassociate ourselves from Frost. He is out there somewhere in space and time other than ours. It is a sort of experiment we venture—we will let Frost be our guide while all the time keeping hold of what we know ourselves to be. In effect we validate Frost's doubleness—he would keep both roads—he would have his cake and eat it. What seems like a reluctance to let go of one road even in the face of absolute necessity is not unlike our own attitude towards the poem. Every time a reader picks up this poem there are then *two roads*, Frost's and the reader's, or the poem's and the poem as read by the reader. Two is a lovely number. It serves Frost well. It is cozy because it encourages intimacy.

If one goes through the poem line by line it is astonishing to note how at any place in the poem we are in a special unique place. One of my assignments is always to move through the poem plotting out Frost's emotional tone or condition, be it dark or light, optimistic, accepting, defiant, regretful, etc. to show that the poem creates for us a dynamic of thought. Thereby the attempt is to discredit the notion that in Frost or in any poetry we can doze off for a while and awake only for the message in the last lines. Long before McLuhan the medium was the message. Waiting for the last lines is an insult not only to Frost but to oneself—we are not going to be so stupid as to let Frost get away with so much before the poem is over. Or we are going to be that most experiential person who has nothing to trust but experience, and so demands to experience the poem line by line, syllable by syllable. Proof for this is easily available. If one parachutes down into line 8, for instance, the road under consideration is "grassy and wanted wear," as if this made it different. Of if we consider the famous second to last line—"I took the one less traveled by," we get only a partial sense of the whole poem—in this instance a totally wrong notion.

One of the more idle questions I used to plague myself with and which I finally discarded because it seemed irrelevant is "Why are there two roads and not three? Or more?" I've come to intersections of five roads, out driving, and while dangerous they are also quite exciting for the sudden imposition of all these opportunities. Does number matter? Having no choice at all is different from having a choice, and maybe that's the basic distinction. We in America make a lot of living in a system which gives us two candidates, one

Reagan, one Mondale, as infinitely superior to being offered only Chernenko or Stalin. Still, even for the Russians, we can always seek another alternative, not to like either, or not to like that we *have to* choose. Frost, however, does not reserve the right to refuse either, though he does "keep the first for another day." Imagining a plenitude of choices—if one goes far enough—is to get beyond human limits—to force on oneself the mind of God. Or is to imagine the universe as a multitude too vast for comprehension, thereby leading us to a very different vision of things. This "vision" may also be a poetic vision, but it is one devoid of ego or irony. I lapse into this vision from time to time—good times all—to sit in rapt wonder at infinity. I feel like one of fifty zillion pebbles on a beach. Frost's "two" while seemingly much narrower, opens up into an infinity of sorts because it opens to thesis/antithesis, good and evil, right and wrong, life and death, "things in pairs ordained to everlasting opposition." We are in that vague world of moral quandaries which can be as huge a morass as being abandoned to sheer vastness. Whatever apology we want to make, Frost's dilemma is more than adequate for him or for us. I halfway imagine a poem with the same title which has as its text only the first line— "Two roads diverged in a yellow wood." And all those who are in the know, or who "are in enough on the game," smile outwardly and inwardly the same. Stuck up on a banner we can see it flying over the Robert Frost express—whirlwind tour of America—slogan and banner, or on a sweatshirt properly bedraggled and threadbare to indicate another who went and tried and did his best and who will perish with the rest. I was defeated by two roads, the one I took, the one I didn't take, sometimes the one I took more at me, sometimes the other. When I died, I died for both.

Frost might have ended his poem with a period at the end of the first line as much to say "Forgive Oh Lord my little jokes on thee/And I'll forgive Thy great big one on me."—but Frost is early here and has a lot to say, or has not yet pushed in earnest to formulate what won't formulate, what won't formulate in poems reduced to punch lines at a party. There is still the need to heed the feel of the going, the physical and mental fluxion of it all. Frost's life is not to be entered in evidence by footnote—we are not yet so much in on the joke—Frost's intimacy with us is not a forsworn conclusion. And yet it is of course by poems like this that Frost moved toward that coziness which gave him the security to render reality in couplets detached from body and soul. And poems like these, if we care to know, Frost started every reading with. Though he ended with grace notes and jokes. "The Road Not Taken" is, with others like it, his apprenticeship in life. And so it is fair to ask of it what we would ask of any poem—how does it make itself a world, a sufficiency, a reality to momentarily displace us from our own and hold us for a little while.

And so it is two roads. And two that split from one is a real problem for those of us who know within our essential beings that we are either here or there. So there is an appeal right away to what is practical—that it is true we cannot "travel both." Frost is eminently reasonable. He presents the facts, and there is a nice factual feel to this poem—

Two roads diverged in a yellow wood

Number and color—not some vague fantastic blurry world a poet drunk on wine or words might want to pass off as our world. Coupled with a next line that admits limit and also a degree of regret—"And sorry I could not travel both." We seem safely on our way to an altogether sane explanation of what, where, when, how and why. Frost's approach is, in an important sense, practical and thorough. There is no tearing of hair. Instead with steady eye and hand, and in a voice slack of emotion that borders on monotony or indifference he sets out:

And be one traveler, long I stood
And looked down one as far as I could
To where it bent in the undergrowth;

It would be easier, I think, if a poem like this would start out strong and sure and then get into trouble somewhere, but there are many kinds of strength and many kinds of trouble. Is there a line in Frost more sure in stress than this first one which is yet, in naming of predicament, more his undoing. We feel the weight fall hard on "Two" and "roads" and then the wondrous word "diverged," a verb stressed on its second syllable as if it cocked itself to spring at us from firm ground. Three out of the first four syllables are stressed. Let there be no doubt! There were two roads and they diverged. The second part of the line is flimsy in contrast, as if it shies away from what emphasis has been made. The preposition and article skitter along in a hurry to the first syllable of "yellow" which then seems sure again only to dissipate its energy and confidence as its second syllable falls away to "wood," which in some readings firms again as its place in the line would have it, but is rather shaky finally as if it never quite gets over wearing such a loud up-front adjective as "yellow." And so on.

"Sorry" in the next line pairs up with "yellow"—the wood is yellow and I was sorry—as if this is one of the secret answers to this poem—for those who see its sorrow as autumnal. Generally Frost's lines are uncomfortable unless they are even-numbered and come out even. TRNT wants to be iambic, tetrameter or pentameter, but always falls short or long by one syllable. This is important because it is the iambic base from which Frost launches his missions into the unknown. "Diverged" is a sufficient clue because it is an iambic foot unto itself, so if we don't know how to read "Two roads" the next word leans by a kind of backwards hearing to keep the line properly firm. A poem like TRNT is about Frost's poetry as much as it is about poetry in general or about whatever truth there is to be found in the world. And if the poem looks back in its title, and if it looks ahead to look back in its final stanza, we are also made to hear backwards by the overwhelming presence of "diverged." The stress structure of "diverged" then partially remakes "Two roads" into an iambic foot, but as if it exhausted itself in that enterprise it cannot order out iambic marching in the last five syllables. Therefore the first syllable of "yellow" gets grabbed up into the convenient anapest and then the iambic to end with. Words like "yellow" or rather phrases like "yellow wood" resist being fractured against some law to yield a pattern. Readers have often noted that this poem is not strong in the feel of a season and this is so because "yellow" gets broken across two separate feet and so loses some of its potency. The first stanza then, despite its reasonable tone, contains within it the inherent awkwardness of the nine-syllable line, five of them in all, with the odd syllable kicking around inside the lines like a loose electron, flashing a little as the last syllable of "traveler," and then in line 4 providing the energy that keeps "as far as I could" together as a phrase, atomic binding as opposed to iambic regularity.

Which means that by this time in his poetry Frost is no longer just a poet of the line. He is beginning to be a poet of the sentence—which he later gloriously becomes, while in the process finding out that the inherent recognizability of colloquial expressions permits the naturalness of speech sounds to freshen a poetic language and meter which sounds stilted if it too much sticks to its rules. Phrase becomes the vehicle by which poetry comes close to voice and to thought—or how the language of thought ceases to be a language foreign from experience.

Two odds will make an even. Either five is long or four is short. Lines balanced five and five as syllables go might give us the classic pentameter. Frost further funs with us by pushing the lines on out to five per stanza, thereby necessitating three end words to sound the "wood" sound.

Readings of this sort can be made to prove anything. You just decide what you want to show and the poem gives up its evidence—a sort of universal donor. But what I am trying to say should not be anything but obvious—it is more or less a principle of life—that there is instability within stability, or there is stability even as there is instability. To say this, however, we must realize that for poetry this is high praise. And that furthermore we are revealing what comes to us not from the forthright message of the poem but from its formal qualities. At the same time I want to say let's call the structure of the poem part of the rational or willed dimension—since will becomes—what one shall will himself to say—so much essential to the fullest statement of the poem. This poem can comfort us as all Frost's poems can and do by the recurrence of rhyme and the re-establishment of meter. For instance, in stanza two, whatever deviation we get in the early half of the lines, Frost restores iambic regularity in the last four syllables in every line. We have "as just as fair," "the better claim," "and wanted wear," "the passing there," and "about the same." This restored meter is accompanied by strong end stops to the lines, with only one that runs over, whereas in the first stanza, three lines are enjambed.

Meter offers comfort, but Frost is a restless soul. If it is with "outer playfulness then with inward seriousness," or something like that, as he tells it. Or let's let him be more mischievous—one thing works so that another can fail. It is a sort of law of compensation, which may, through various perverse permutations, declare Frost's inherent contrariness as craftsman and thinker. Or it is to say that poems are imperfect. But not for want of trying. Nor is it Frost who makes them imperfect. It is the meaning we want to attach to it. I say rhyme fails in its duty to pull us wide and then back as rhymes can in a stanza where the sounds are markedly different. But this is not true of stanza two of TRNT. All five end words are more alike than they are different. *Fair* and *claim* and *wear* and *there* and *same* could pass for rhyme words all together in the same poem, all "a" rhymes, where something else would be the "b" sound. Something similar operates in stanza one with the "o" sound. Is the "o" to be, in an equation, the sound of the first road, and the "a" sound the second? We do very much notice the change—we hear it emphatically as Frost, having done all he can with the first road, leaps through the stanza break to the second—

> To where it bent in the undergrowth;
> (space)
> Then took the other, as just as fair,

This kind of turning or swerving away from what has been posited or established to something else is one of the great pleasures of TRNT. And the turn is almost a physical turning. The sudden decision to take the other, which begins stanza two, is to me a powerful release, a sudden commitment dramatized powerfully in Frost's choice to break for a stanza. By the time we get to the line end we feel a new wind in the poem, a new sound. This is a wonderful phenomenon common to many of his poems, where through rhythm or stanza break, change of pace or change of rhyme we are given the illusion of being new, of starting again. Here, of course, a big assist goes to the sequential quality of the telling—this poem is as much a narration as a meditation. All those sounds associated with the first road, finalized in "undergrowth," are suddenly left behind, and it is as if we had in fact left the dilemma behind as well, come as it were out of woods into a clear place. The exhilaration we feel is due also I think to Frost's verbs "diverged" and "bent," two strong verbs, the former especially effective as noted earlier. Both imply a bending away or turning down or away, almost a kind of cocking motion, the way we work against a spring storing up its energy toward a sudden climactic release. Both are the property of the roads, which we might call Frost's antagonists. In contrast the protagonist is decidedly passive—he is "sorry," he stands "long" in one place, he looks. We cannot tell what is going to happen, but from lines three to five we see the narrator looking over the first road. Presumably he will list its attributes and then turn to examine, in a similar way, the second. This is not what happens, of course, and were we not so used to this poem we might better be able to remark the originality Frost shows, how truly daring he is, how amidst considerations and rather cool analysis Frost's reckless spirit takes over.

The move from stanza one to stanza two is a memorable one, where the poet is mastered not by logic or reason but by impulse. That he gets reasonable again, and analytical, even before the line is over, demonstrates Frost's other attractive quality, his essential reasonableness. But in one line the two come together, and there probably is no other line in all his poetry where the two can be seen more intensely balanced. A proper analogue for what Frost does here might come from athletics—the high jumper leaps hugely over a bar from a slow deliberate approach, with all his energy focussed in the leap upwards against the downward tug of gravity and oblique to his own forward motion. Half a second later the jumper is on his feet again on the other side balancing the scales of justice in his steady hands. So Frost escapes the tug of the first road, the inertia he's under from having been stalled out at the fork. It's like a rocket escaping our atmosphere—that "took" that Frost says so simply. Whereupon, almost immediately, in the interval the comma provides, Frost restores the poised considerate tone of the first stanza. The effect is startling, to be sure, that this poet so much associated with easy-going countrified wisdom and a deliberate careful posing could strike so swiftly.

The second half of the first line of the second stanza is rather awkward but usually isn't noted for being so. Were this poem an earlier poem and more riddled with inversions and poetic contractions and diction or archaic words "as just as fair" would be just another license the poet is taking. Here we can breeze by it unaware of how strange a phrase it is. Maybe the momentum accrued by Frost's taking the second road, catching us off balance as he does, or because we are so startled as we are, keeps us from noticing. "As just as fair" is not normal usage. No one talks like this. We have, of course, "just as fair," but the other "as" is unnecessary, and might be there simply to pad out the line so the iambic meter will work better, meter that needs to work in order to cover up other shenanigans. But there is a precedent for this phrase as phrase in stanza one which prepares us for it—the phrase "as far as I could" with its two appearances of "as" in the same positions. "As far as" softens us up for "as just as" the former being so recognizable as to be nearly a cliché, the latter so strange as to make us wonder where the poet got his English. But TRNT is a poem of balances, the balancing act the mind must achieve in order to live, and effects a balance here between the overly familiar and the totally new. Certainly the freshness we feel in Frost comes in part from this balance, from this tension between the stale and very casual and colloquial and related expression which confirms the poet as a speaker of our native tongue, and those odd dislocations and reaches into zones heretofore forbidden, in this case the space for permutation very near the colloquial. "As just as fair" comes in to fill the space prepared for by "as far as I," and fits it perfectly as meter is concerned. Resident here as well, within the cloud or echo chamber of associated choices, is "just as far," which is another base to build off variations from. And there may be other things nearby as well. What we get, in sum, is the reflection or partial reflection of similar things, voice and echo, or partial echo, reinforcement with variation, the old and true revitalized by the fresh and new, the poet as he who finds among our words the words to tell us in a poet's tongue the words we know, to polish them off and give them back to us, and the poet of another realm, a new place, new voice, one whose daring or strangeness of view will lead us toward new opportunities for word and deed.

The unity of "as just as fair" with "as far as I" is akin to Frost's choice of situation and scene for their symbolic portent. The two roads imply choice and difference, and carry the weight of consequence. He will work with these connotations and very close to them—the way Hemingway praises a matador for working so close to the horns of the bull. Meanwhile Frost profits from the appearance of compliance within a pattern that formulates. Similarly Frost's echoes and variations, his laying down one phrase as a road upon which to push a different yet similar one, keeps us in the poem even while giving Frost freedom. The combination of phrases gives us the uncanny feeling that we are hearing what we have already heard or already know but never said quite so well or quite this way. Was this what we know? Is this how we knew it? Barring the interruption that never comes, the objection no one delivers, the poem transpires amidst our grateful recognition and acceptance even as we know there is something unusual about it. Frost's best poems are nearly always cases of deja vu.

"As just as fair" is curious in another way, or provides a service that is above and beyond what is either required or desired—a sweet abundance which is common to Frost's greatest poems, the giving beyond our poor power to repay or acknowledge. With two roads under consideration "just" is to one what "fair" is to the other. This phrase, while awkward in syntax, formulates neatly in the language of mathematical equivalencies. "As just" is equal to "as fair," and as we read the line we feel Frost's mind working toward balance. He had just expressed his having taken the "other" road, now he sets out to explain or justify it. One could say he's heaping it up pretty high, the "other" he chooses is both *just* and *fair* while also being "just as fair" as the first. So in the process of making such claims he sets out in graphic terms the equation which will later haunt the careless reader—the undeniable equivalence of the roads. One can also talk about compression, how "as just as fair" is a poetry shorthand for what in prose might be "which was just as fair," so that we imagine an apostrophe just before the "as" of the first "as" to indicate that "which wa-" has been omitted for purposes of syllable count and meter. Such is Robert Frost's breathtaking inventiveness.

We are barely into the poem. Many riches lie ahead. I have already noted the pleasure of leaving behind, which is what we experience when the "o" of *both* and *stood* and *growth* and *wood* become the "a" of *fair* and *claim*. And this pleasure of leaving behind in a poem which seems significantly about the difficulty of letting go. But there is also the pleasure of staying with, of looking and holding and saying and staying so as to keep, to make one's own, the pleasure of being thorough. Frost is incredibly various, incredibly talented, incredibly divided amidst and against himself—and who pulls us off in many directions at once so that reading him becomes equivalent to being alive in ourselves at moments of urgency when we need all our wits about us. The pleasure of staying with is already present in how Frost pushes the rhymes in stanza one and two. We can also look ahead to Frost's running the a of *fair* and *claim* into its more pure unalloyed form in "lay" and "day" in stanza three. There is another manifestation of staying in Frost's obsession with the "as" sound of the word "as" and its cousins. Line 4 of the first stanza introduces "as" and gives it a second hearing, but the sound proliferates in the second stanza. The word "as" occurs three times, is incorporated into "was," dominates "grassy" and "passing," occurs partly muted in "because" and is then fractured into "perhaps." In addition the "a" of "as" is voiced in "and" and "wanted" and "that" and "Had." A careful look back into stanza one shows a similar domination of "o" words with "roads" and "yellow" and "wood " and "could" and "one" and "long" and "looked" and "down" and "To" etc. with the persistence of the "o" embodying Frost's attention to the dilemma and the examination of the first road. So Frost trades one persistence for another. There is, I think, an extraordinary attentiveness in this display—almost a friendliness. It is as if the poet gives over the extent of one of his resources to the addressing of the problem. A more widely-distributed employing of vowels might likewise be taken as a marshalling of resources, but working in such tight spaces as Frost is such a thing would probably be seen as meaningless or at best random. Such concentration of sound indicates concentration of mind. One of Frost's strengths is always how his poems seem finished, accomplished. It is rare that a reader of a poem, no matter what its length, finds the poem over too soon or insufficiently developed. We don't fault Frost for abandoning his poems or failing to properly consider the implications of the subject or situation. There is, instead, nearly always the conviction that he has been thorough, that he has made a credible and even sometimes an exhaustive investigation. The role played by the persistence of like sounds cannot be overestimated. Another way to demonstrate this saturation and the spell it creates is to examine a word like "grassy" (in which the "as" sound is strong) for its normal image-making capacity. In a poem as weak as this one is in images we would expect "grassy" to make a strong impression. It has little to compete with— "undergrowth" being its most vital predecessor. "Yellow wood" is somewhat vivid, but it is bothered by its abstractive tendency—"woods" would seem possessed more of actual trees. "Leaves," which follows it, doesn't get into the poem until four lines later, in another stanza, and are themselves denied by the curious syntax of their line: "In leaves no step had trodden black." Other words in stanza two, be they nouns or adjectives, are determinedly not physical: *other, fair, claim, wear, passing,* and so on, which thereby might help set off "grassy" through contrast. Also, by advantage of position, the word occurs in the exact geographic center of the stanza, occupying as it does syllables four and five of the nine syllables in line 3. Otherwise the word is also prominent by stress, its first syllable taking the one accent in the anapest which builds through *it* and *was*. And in terms of how we read the sense of the stanza it bears the burden of showing how the "claim" is perhaps "better," and so is awaited with considerable expectation. But it turns out to be a huge disappointment because the word is hardly heard at all as a unique thing. Instead it is part of the splendid music of variations on its dominant sounds. Frost's insistence on the power of sound is worth noting: "The ear is the only true writer and the only true reader," he tells us, and stanza two gives us ear writing with a vengeance. Sound moves from its component aspect to the forefront of our attention, and Frost's. One is tempted to say he got so fascinated by the sounds of the words he forgot to show how the roads were different, which he once seemed sure of, and which, he later, upon no evidence, claims. Sound shows like this are common in Frost but not always so subtle or so lavish. There are more extreme examples, though, in places in "An Old Man's Winter Night" and "The Sound of Trees," where hearing the poems without the text in front of us produces a different text, where the sounds sometimes ascend purely as musical notes devoid of sure meaning.

At a place like this in a poem like this it is almost imperative to say that poetry takes over from the intelligence, that the joy of sound for its own sake takes precedence over the search for attitude or truth. Or that Frost becomes nearly all ear, not just listening at a door beyond which words are spoken whose import cannot be determined, but speaks himself in both the sound of sense and the sounds of sensation. Such a condition cannot be pushed too far; it breaks down into something less responsible than poetry claims for itself. It breaks down naturally, as metaphor breaks down eventually, and the trick is always to fill the cup up to the brim and even above the brim, to push to a limit of bounty and fullness. And so it is not that "grassy" makes no contribution for image. It

Greg Kuzma

does. As it must in a poem about roads in a wood, which needs be physical enough to make a scene we can believe in.

Frost's obsession with sound is balanced by his obsession with meaning. Ultimately. In the great poems the joys of one are kept equal with the joys of the other. The worst of Frost's poems are opinions, no more than that, attitudinizing, boorish, where his ego takes over and he becomes himself the victim of his own self confidence. How words sound no longer matters—what matters is that he has important things to say. Letting the Bard develop as he did was the worst thing that could have happened to the precarious beauty of his poetry.

Frost's holding sounds, holding the same sounds, as he does in stanza two, I have called the pleasure of staying. It is to savor one's own words, to delight in the gift of speech, the physical essence of language and its reality as sound. In a poem like this it is also that talk of considerations which delays the movement on, in time, a way of forestalling the inevitable. Some of the great power of this poem resides in this aspect—that once the dilemma of the first line is asserted, and its implications accepted—which the second line establishes—one has no choice, as it were, but to go forward on one road or the other. So Frost's weighing and measuring take on the dignity of last words, words aware of their mortal content. I overdo this somewhat, of course, but in a poem which is as tricky and playful as this it's remarkable how its overall tone is so sober and weary. There really is no mystery about it—"The Road Not Taken" is written by a man already very much aware of loss, of time's erosions, in a New England whose glory had all but faded, whose own youthful dreams had been diminished.

There are no illusions. The look backward with which the poem begins does not commend us to a childhood of delight and sensation or security, "of a time made simple by the loss of detail," nor does the look ahead into the future offer comfort except how he will establish a sense of commitment through an act of his own will. Nor is there right or wrong. The abiding truths are there—within the poem—we are physically limited in what we can do—we cannot take both roads, let alone five or six. When we come to use our senses we can

see only a short ways, where then even undergrowth defies
our gaze; when we do act we must act on impulse and justify
things afterwards. Or try as hard as we can to see distinctions,
physical reality defies us—there is finally no choice but to
accept whatever it is we are. It is not that Frost cannot affect
confidence—line 13 is thick with bravado—"Oh I kept the
first for another day." But it is undercut immediately by the
knowledge he already has acquired—"how way leads on to
way," which is what the situation of the forked road is in
the act of further demonstrating. Whether Frost is heroic in
the face of these realities, or just matter of fact, whether he
is having fun at the expense of all those of us who expect
life to have purpose and meaning, or fun at the instinct for
making poems with statements to live by, is up for grabs. The
real choice in TRNT is not the speaker's but the reader's, or
the reader's and the poet's to the extent the reader will share
an understanding of the poem as an act itself which is as
important and meaningful as any decision one might make
in life.

What I am working towards is something like this—
TRNT creates the illusion that it will formulate reality for us,
but then fails to do so. It then suggests that *it is what we make
of it* that is our only recourse. In the final stanza Frost steps
forward in time out of a present that is essentially implied
merely by the existence of his voice—or, before we begin
reading the poem itself as document—something which
exists and can be found and read. What Frost tells us in his
projected hindsight is essentially an untruth, a statement
that derives not at all from the circumstances as he presents
them earlier. Why the lie? Is Frost trying to dramatize that
necessary belief in ourselves we all have, our essential validity
even though we make no important contribution on behalf
of good or nothing against evil? I think so. TRNT is a poem
in praise of the splendor of mere being. The famous "sigh"
is an oh-so-gentle reminder not only of regret for all that
has not been but also for what "ages and ages," time itself,
does to us, and how little any time is in the continuum of
vast and endless time. So we feel how small the poet is—who
is—telling this: how lovely that pause at the end of the third

to the last line, where all the burden of time and thought and care and loss rests suddenly upon him—will he be broken by it? Will he be brought to silence in the face of what he knows? There is a moment when we do not know what will happen, when were we there and hearing it aloud read to us by its author we might not know if he could go on or not. Such a moment came at last for Frost, ages and ages after he wrote this poem, at the Kennedy inaugural. There the road he took got lost in the undergrowth and only by stepping back to some earlier road could he speak. The pause at the end of the line sets down the prophecy Frost's life fulfilled.

What Frost's speaker makes of life is not very much. Either he mocks his rationalization of one road over the other, or he knows he will in fact believe it. Curiously the conventional notion that the end of the poem establishes Frost's preference for poetry over some other vocation becomes, ironically, a real possibility. It is, of course, an available option that any poem about perception is an alternative as itself in any choice of what the poem tells us.

It's just as conventional to say Frost's poem, while trying to find sure meaning in the world fails, in one sense, to do so while, in another sense, establishes in its resonant and beautiful language a thing of value, a meaning to live by, poetry itself. And so "The Road Not Taken" is a call to poetry, an invitation into the mysterious and beautiful dream of words.

Down, But Not Out—
Robert Frost Meets
The Oven Bird (And He Is It)

"The Oven Bird" is not one of Frost's greatest poems. But it is skillfully made, if not exquisitely made, and even perhaps tighter and more economic than the other sonnets. One might call its economy an index to its theme, or say that its economy is amplified through the theme to enhance its overall effect. Or one might say that its workmanlike quality is an emotional clue to where in the psyche the poem has its proper place. I do not in any way think the poem to be minor. Frost's minor poems, as we understand the word, are far too frequently flawed poems. There is something that is compromised in them—meter being made to force a gap, or some too-obvious rhyme, but more typically an atmosphere of sentimentality that we cannot abide, and that we do not find in the serious poems. "The Oven Bird" is entirely serious. It is a poem expressive of Frost's most pervasive theme—what to make of loss and diminishment, a theme that is not only Frost's major contribution to poetry but perhaps poetry's most universal and prevalent concern. And "The Oven Bird" is precisely *the* poem which, in its most expressively literal language, gives the best statement in the fewest number of words of this theme. So when we are looking around for some distillation of Frost's obsessive concerns in his best poems, we invariably blunder across and come to embrace the last line of the poem. To a very real extent the very obviousness, the very deliberateness, the plain directness of the statement, is everything that is wrong with it. Poetry, we are apt to say, should not know itself so well. Or no self-respecting poet leaves lying around such a bald and naked declaration of his most obsessive theme. And so it has been customary, habitual, to use "The Oven Bird" as a gloss upon the other poems, to refer to it in a footnote—as a footnote—and hardly ever to examine it in and for itself. I would like, here, in these pages, to study the poem with a more full expectation that it has a bounty to yield if only we might come to it openly.

The Oven Bird

There is a singer everyone has heard,
Loud, a mid-summer and a mid-wood bird,
Who makes the solid tree trunks sound again.
He says that leaves are old and that for flowers
Mid-summer is to spring as one to ten.
He says the early petal-fall is past
When pear and cherry bloom went down in showers
On sunny days a moment overcast;
And comes that other fall we name the fall.
He says the highway dust is over all.
The bird would cease and be as other birds
But that he knows in singing not to sing.
The question that he frames in all but words
Is what to make of a diminished thing.

I have been reading this poem and attempting to talk about
it for at least ten years, perhaps longer. At times, especially when
I have been enthusiastic about "Hyla Brook" or "Mowing,"
"The Oven Bird" has seemed somewhat in the shadows of these
more passionate poems, sort of a second cousin but one less
well born, less lucky. Its placement in *The Complete Poems of
1949* has also made me, perhaps involuntarily, subordinate it to
"Hyla Brook."

"The Oven Bird" follows "Hyla Brook" on the next page, and
is the flip-side, if you will, of it, the way 45 rpm records always
had less desirable songs on the backs of the songs we bought the
records for. Given the great beauty of and abundance of "Hyla
Brook," its overflow into an extra line being the primary proof
of its transcendence, its showpiece language, musical images, its
impoverished opening circumstances incredibly rescued at the
very last by a wonderfully exuberant affirmation, "The Oven
Bird" seems bleak and plain and flat and dull, and maybe even
anti-poetical. It is as if Frost, in writing the two poems together,
poured all his genius and enthusiasm into the former, and had
only bits and pieces to make a mere perfunctory assemblage
of the latter. A very worthwhile study might be made of the
two together—they have much in common as mirror images,

as question and corresponding reply, as presence and absence, as complements of each other, as echoes of each other, and finally perhaps as bookends to that long shelf of poems amongst which we would have no choice but to include such masterpieces as "Spring Pools," "Desert Places," "The Onset," "The Need of Being Versed in Country Things," "After Apple Picking," indeed, all these and the other supreme and unforgettable performances. And yet so often the poem seems hurried to me, and hasty, again, in contrast to "Hyla Brook" or "Mowing," where richness of diction, polysyllabic words, and their penchant for sentences that become fat with the accumulation of many pleasures, gives these poems a bulkiness which looms them large and full and thick. "The Oven Bird" looks starved in contrast, emaciated. Held up to the light— backing "Hyla Brook" as it does—the poem looks to be not only a line short, which it is, but maybe even two, maybe not even a whole and proper sonnet. And reading it aloud, year after year, one must remark how soon it comes to say its say and be done. But everything is relative, most definitely in Frost, the poet of so many presumed absolutes. Just as the great power of "Hyla Brook" is born from the least likely of scenes, the most depleted spirits, so the true genius of "The Oven Bird" is made clear in its own true time.

The poem begins without fanfare. Frost calls us to attend upon the presence of a bird which he says "everyone has heard." The first line is almost an apology. This is, I think, a dangerous maneuver. The business of poetry has nearly always involved if not Poe's supernal beauty then heightened states at least. "Mowing," we can note, begins with an overdeveloped portentousness, and so is rather a traditional poem in this regard. "The Oven Bird" invites neglect. The singer is question is all too familiar. He is not exotic, not rare, not even easily comparable to the notion of the poet as singer since poets are, or used to be, few among the masses of men and women. But as I say this I realize that the line has two thrusts, not just one, and that I am pursuing only one of them. The phrase "everyone has heard" may indeed invite yawns, on one hand, but, heard differently, it carries equally well the opposite meaning. A bird "everyone has heard" is a bird we all know, and, by implication, are not averse to know. Such a bird may bring us together, unite us in a shared experience of the world, the way the robin in Spring releases in us all a glad sense of renewal. We are not, then, it seems, to be brought special private insights made valid only through the fervor of the poet's experience. This song need not be authenticated by experts, nor must we suspend disbelief. It is to be available to all, like sunlight or rain. One is tempted to go on waxing poetic to the possibilities except that what we have, in fact, is an irresolvable ambiguity. Is the bird boringly familiar and not easy to listen to again, and maybe not worth listening to, or is it some ubiquitous and universal melody indistinguishable from the very life force itself, from our own breathing or heartbeat. The problem is very real, and made the more irritating by the very flatness of the line. To speak in a plain voice—and this is as plain a voice as Frost ever manages—to seek the path of fewest entanglements, fewest overtones or nuances, and yet to be in so much trouble so soon. The first line of "Mowing" calls attention to itself in numerous ways—the first line of "Hyla Brook" also. The first line of "The Oven Bird" seems to seek the lesser road, not to parade exclusiveness, not to affirm the value of the personal, but to address the general and the pleasantly familiar. Frost's attitude toward his material is always a problem. Usually, however, the problem is an ultimate one, one we don't feel the need to consider until at the last, after the poem is over and done. By raising so much up so soon Frost brands "The Oven Bird" with a special originality, and by doing so also forces upon the reader a degree of scrutiny and attentiveness that all but insures the reader's active participation in the poem. Whether or not the ambiguity is resolvable, and I'm not sure it can be, such canny writing carries with it a measure of mystery and wonder which we associate only with the poem that pushes against the limits of language and knowledge. So, almost inadvertently, perhaps inadvertently, "The Oven Bird" becomes a poem that cannot escape significance. It is as if doomed to it.

As much as I would like to leave behind comparisons to "Hyla Brook" and "Mowing" for a while, at least, ere it seem it is they I really prefer, yet as first lines go "The Oven Bird" bears a striking resemblance to "Mowing." I would also like to be relieved of having to deal with Frost's ambiguity. But I have become committed to the struggle. "Mowing"'s "never" we remark for its exclusiveness and for how it draws all that considerable attention upon itself. "Everyone" works seemingly to an opposite effect. Instead of a situation known only to the poet and for the significance of which we await his pronouncements, we have a situation for which we almost have no need for a poet at all. This may later be important when we come to realize how totally Frost has left the scene for the bird to interpret. "The Oven Bird" resembles "Mowing" then in this regard also, that much of what is revealed or discovered or posited springs from sources ostensibly other than the poet. In fact, "The Oven Bird" is rather quite extreme in this because the poet's "I" never appears at all. It might be fair to suggest that the "I" is present in the poem as an implied component of the "everyone," which, interestingly, also includes then ourselves. I am beginning to get close to posing the paradox of the "everyone." I said earlier that Frost's "never"—in being restrictive and categorical, sharpens our attention—we read the poem for proof of its claim. "Everyone," as it turns out, is just as much an extravagance. Statistically or otherwise it is just as impossible to prove a "never" as it is an "everyone." One exception in either case destroys the thesis. But "everyone" has a dimension "never" doesn't have. It is large and generous and democratic and all-embracing. Instead of provoking our doubt, raising our probability hackles, it brings the tendency for relaxing us, causing us to lower our guards, accept more readily than we might have otherwise the assertions Frost will make in the poem. This is a tricky and daring business, but it brings us to the heart of one of the real dimensions of this poem. In accepting "everyone" we extend our consent, and it is upon this consent that Frost builds the apparent truthfulness of the experience. We become co-authors with Frost. This may be precisely why the poem seems to transpire so smoothly and so rapidly for us; so much of it may occur before we become re-alerted to our separateness, to our role as audience. And this may explain how a poem of this consummate skill might lay concealed, hidden so long within the body of the poet's work. Poems like "Mending Wall" or "Birches" we have no trouble reading: Frost is fully present, person and persona, and nearly everything that occurs is brought home to him for his sorting out, signature or commentary. In "The Oven Bird" the ego of the poet is never engaged. It is as if the insights, the lessons, the very voice, comes from some secret source in the world.

What is the voice of the oven bird? Readers who don't like this poem are quick to complain that Frost offers many possible interpretations of it without really ever establishing it in the first place. All these repetitions of "He says" are not the bird talking but Frost. A problem then becomes whether or not Frost's view of the bird's dark meanings is something he imposes, something that is his far more than it is the world's. This problem arises always when we try to see ourselves in nature, whether we look there for vindication or kinship or the faintest glimmer of likeness. When are we reading in? When are we jumping to conclusions? How much are we projecting our own moods and needs onto blank and indifferent trees and animals? These questions are serious ones in Frost, even though he may not always raise them directly. Frequently the assumption is that nature does have much to tell us not only about itself but about ourselves. Usually this is couched in "the need of being versed in country things," where the poet is one of those "in on the game," sharing the wisdom of people who live close to the earth. But this is for me too homespun a guise Frost wears, too much a cheery regional dialect. While there are many successful poems written in this posture, many strongly bound up in Frost's personality as New Englander, "The Oven Bird" is far more audacious and original. One must admire its directness, its boldness, its refusal to take on a tone which might lighten its dark burden. One must admire, as well, how it anticipates the objections of its detractors and answers them. For instance, those who complain that the bird is not like the usual birds, will be agreed with. This is no spring singer of beautiful songs. Were the oven bird a brook it would be Hyla Brook, the brook without water in it, full of weeds and dirt. The link with "Hyla Brook" is irresistible. Frost celebrates here as he does in the other poem one of the neglected, the ignored, the unlovely. The poem also answers the criticism that Frost is really making all this up—that there really is no oven bird in nature whose voice lends itself to any such interpretations, and that Frost's poem is all assertions of meaning but never any real presentation of the sound of the bird. In speaking about "Mowing" in another essay, I worked to make a case for the presence of the sound of the scythe within the sound of the words of the poem. No less a case is possible here. In fact, the poems are really quite similar in that in both Frost sees the problem as one that needs to be dispensed with early on—almost every component of the sound of the scythe makes appears in the opening two lines. So too for "The Oven Bird." The key words are the couplet rhymes in the first two lines, but they are assisted by "Loud" in the lead-off position in line 2, and by the repetition of "mid" words, "mid-summer" and "mid-wood" also in line 2. "Loud" is most certainly *loud*. After the iambic flow in line 1 our expectation points to a less-stressed syllable to lead off the second line as well. Behind line 1's five iambic feet for precedent lies the greater precedent of Frost's near-total commitment to iambic lines in his poetry. But if that is not enough to make "Loud" loud, Frost also follows the word with a comma. Such a rare thing it is for him or anyone to pause so strongly after a single lead-off syllable in a line, the comma is read more as an exclamation mark than as a comma. But the major contribution of language to making the sound of the bird comes from the "ur" sounds and "d" sounds of the couplet rhyme words "heard" and "bird." These "ur" sounds (along with the "u" of "summer" and the "oo" of "wood") are not happy sounds. Saying them our mouths are drawn closed or down, our lips closing, our teeth nearly shut. These are in no way the open-throated songs of Spring's renewal and rebirth and joy. Some might say that "song" is not a fitting word for such dark music. And it is interesting that the poem addresses itself to this objection also in going on to show a stretching against the usual limits of the word, or using the word ironically. Frost's bird here is one more out of Poe than out of Shelley—it has Poe's doom and gloom in its motif. If one thinks of another famous dark bird, Stevens's blackbird, the resemblance is uncanny—"the blackbird whirled in the autumn winds." Stevens and Frost are using the same sounds.

Frost does a nice job of getting caught up in and getting us caught up in his description. If "loud" is not what we are usually looking for in a bird, mid-summer is not the time, either, when birds are important to us. Neither is mid-wood a place overly familiar—we would tend to avoid such places for fear of getting lost. Neither do birds seem plentiful in the woods. Trees and shadows all but obscure them from sight. Even though the word "mid-summer" tends to prepare us for "mid-wood," Frost is really taking us far afield. If we can rely on a poet's other poems for guidance, the more-famous poem "The Wood-Pile" comes readily to mind. There the poet gets lost in the woods, and is rescued, more or less, by a bird that leads him along, if not astray, until he discovers the wood-pile's provocative presence and symbol. The part of the poem useful to "The Oven Bird" is the great to-do Frost makes of staggering around in the woods, how it is an uncomfortable activity, especially in winter. There is the closed-in feeling, it's hard to know where one is, except "far from home." The summer woods is not much better—witness "Birches," where "life is too much like a pathless wood/ Where your face burns and tickles with the cobwebs/ Broken across it, and one eye is weeping/ From a twig's having lashed across it open." In nearly all of Frost's poems the woods are difficult places to be in or to try to see from, and one gets the impression that we are to find ourselves in them reluctantly. What "everyone," then, is doing mid-summer in the middle of the woods, is a question the poem doesn't answer. Maybe a poet like Frost comes to resolve certain nagging questions for himself temporarily, and from that brief clarity or cleared space, sets out to explore in new directions. Or perhaps Frost is making another bow in our general direction. We know the oven bird, he tells us, everyone does. Because it is loud, of course, but also because we are not just spring people, not just fair weather types, but more-committed residents of the earth, who know it and accept it in all its seasons. The mid-summer woods become then not so much a forbidding place to be avoided, but a necessary and acceptable part of our reality.

The ambiguity which I began to discuss earlier regarding the opening line of this poem and how we are to understand that line persists through the first three lines, though it shifts its focus. We do not know if we are to greet the oven bird happily, or resignedly, nor do we know if "loud" is nice, or annoying, or if its loudness is what makes us know it, and in line three we do not know to celebrate the solid tree trunks or to lament their triumph over us. Open places in Frost are often symbols for awareness, and closed-in places symbolic of suffocation or confusion or repression. But Frost also writes of the need for retreat, for burrows, for escape and hiding. What the poem seems to need in the opening lines is proof that the poet at least, of all the everyone, knows it. For those of us who read up on what an "oven bird" is Frost's description of its effects is really quite persuasive. The bird spends much of its time on the ground, where it builds its nest, having, perhaps, because of the density of the woods that are its habitat, renounced the usually upper airy regions of light and breeze, leaf and flower. So in line 3 Frost hears the song of the bird as reinforcing its habitat, making the tree trunks, solid already, more solid, more *sound*. The play on "sound" is characteristic of Frost who will, especially in short poems stingy with their words, make each one work hard. The pun extends in the direction of "echo," but also in the direction of "soundness" of body, solidness. There is something else. Tree trunks are the least talkative of those parts of the tree we are intimate with. Branches sway in the wind; we call them limbs, resembling as they do our own limbs. Leaves are like hands that catch the rain and light, or like tongues the wind gives voice to. And so on. Trunks are generally speechless. They do nothing more than connect the deep-sunk searching roots, the firm and holding roots, to the articulate branches and leaves and flowers. Compellingly here Frost celebrates trunks as another neglected element or thing, and we might well remember "Hyla Brook" and the work done there to celebrate the unlovely thing. So the dull and dark mid-wood, that is, from inside out, all tree trunks, will have its singer too. This is then another fulfillment of the opening gesture toward the universal and democratic. Frost is not a terribly dedicated naturalist, or ecologist. But this poem's attentions gain strength as our awareness as to the earth's amazing richness and interdependence deepens.

We are told how even in caves where no light reaches fish live in underground rivers, blind fish, and arthropods walk about in perpetual darkness, without sight, without pigment. Frost's interest here is not with the distantly remote, the microscopic or the strange, but the thrust of the poem is in this direction toward an accommodatingly larger awareness.

The oven bird becomes then the presiding spirit of its darker world, but no less a singer for that. Line 4 introduces us to what the music of this unusual song may be said to carry:

> He says that leaves are old and that for flowers
> Mid-summer is to spring as one to ten—

Lines 4, 5, 6, and 7, and 8, blend a matter-of-fact tone with a statistical and objective accounting, but also contain the only truly lovely passages in the poem:

> He says the early petal-fall is past
> when pear and cherry bloom went down in showers
> On sunny days a moment overcast;

Someone whose interest is in laying all Frost's poems out on a table and looking for clusters or sequences would immediately snap "The Oven Bird" into place right on the last lines of "Spring Pools." Those "trees that have it in their pent-up buds/ To darken nature and be summer woods," did not think twice after all, or if they did, they left it to the oven bird to apologize for them. Dark foliage has triumphed, and we are even past this point as well. The leaves themselves are "old," and if one is to try to reach back all the way to spring, the flowers come to us only at the furthest extent of our recall. Here Frost does something quite original with the standard line. By positioning "flowers" out where he does at the furthest point in the second-longest line, he makes a graphic symbol for the difficulty of retrieving them. It is leaves then that come to mind first in the world where solid tree trunks sound and resound, and flowers are a distant afterthought. Frost's "one to ten" proportion for the ratio of mid-summer to spring is self-consciously alienating. For a poet who doesn't usually approve of "statistical things,"

Frost shows how by mid-summer the lover of beauty has, through continual losses, become like someone stuck in a large apartment building in a city somewhere, to whom numbers are the only means to measure anything. Frost does not do a lot with numbers in this poem—he rarely does—except to show his disenchantment with such approaches to the world. But the ratio here is complementary to and softens the very unusual reference to "highway" later on. If numbers cannot assess beauty, or praise it sufficiently, they may be all we have in our fallen state. Faintly in this poem one hears not just the cyclical doom of blossoms and leaves, but a larger doom beyond the cycle of nature where by number and highway we go to our fate as a people. It is but glanced at, but it is present, as if the poet who worries incessantly for each small incremental fading in the year's turning, and unwilling to be consoled, will not be the fool who does not witness with despair the other fall, the encroaching doom of city and highway over our best most fragile nature.

Lines 6 and 7 recall the fallen lovelies of the petals. The language of the poem changes in these lines. Earlier, and again later, it is utilitarian, more concerned with what is being said, less concerned with how. Overall the poem is, and especially for a sonnet, extremely plain in its language. I suggested earlier that it might even be anti-poetical. Probably the unattractiveness of the poem generally resides in its near-total commitment to unemotional, practical, efficient language at the expense of the pretty or the musical. Of course the case is made for precisely the language Frost uses—reduced circumstances demand a less effusive response—the hard reality of our new austerity does not permit exuberance. Austerity will become quite natural to the poem by the end of it, to the point where an otherwise disappointing word like "thing"—hardly a word to end a sonnet with—hardly a word for someone of Frost's vocabulary—will seem both natural and inevitable. But for now we need the sting of what is lost.

"When pear and cherry bloom went down in showers" is a lovely line, made the more rare and delicate by being, in effect, alone amidst language plain and drab. But the choice of "pear and cherry," which results in something so delectable to our ears, is not merely an extravagance of sound. Frost might have used "apple" in place of "cherry," and it would have fit just as well in the scheme of the meter. But "apple" would have distracted the symbol hunters, and made Frost's wonderful inventive play on "fall" and "fall" too ulterior and too Christian. I'm not saying that Frost disavows such schematology— he plays with it often enough. Probably he is playing with it here too—a little—why else "the other fall"? But his very deliberateness shows the extent of care he exhibits to be explicit about what he means and what he doesn't mean. There are two falls already—Thank you—the one less publicized but perhaps more sad fall of the flowers, which comes first. This is a nice distinction, and one wonders how it is such knowledge has been with us so long and yet has remained unremarked. Of course the fall of the leaves, the other fall, hurts more because it presages winter, prefigures the earth's dying. I'm sure we owe the new year with its *two falls*, where formerly one had been enough to break our hearts, to Frost's elegiac temperament. Reading him in large doses is to encounter one after another lamentation for all that we lose. And yet death is the mother of beauty after all. Never have flower petals been so exquisitely mourned as here. The pairing of "pear" and "cherry" links the words by rhyme, or assonance, which makes a wedding of two otherwise discrete entities, deepening their loss. The rhymed sound is also in itself important because the repeated sound is the word "air," spelled variously, and which gives back to the petals, through sound, some of their delicacy and fragility against the sky. "Went down" is also an interesting phrase for what it echoes from and what it brings to the poem. The phrase is almost always associated with human dying, nearly always with the drama of struggle or battle. Many specific instances can be found in Shakespeare's plays. The king, who first was seen fighting in a given part of the field, later "went down" amongst his attackers. The emotional impact is large, of great loss, of a tragic vision. "In showers" is important too in that it works both as rain showers and showers of themselves— though spring is a time of *rain* there may not be a bit of it in "The Oven Bird." The very passivity with which the poem is written makes me favor the "showers" of self destruction.

And for such a trifle—a moment's "overcast"! Frost achieves all this in only two lines, less than a sentence.

Every poem needs to acquire for itself its own innate structure and semblance of order and security. There are numerous structural elements present here. Sound organizes the opening lines as Frost works to present a valid rendering of the real life sound of the bird. Then the bird's loud and insistent manner is sounded and resounded by way of the three occasions where "He says" initiates sentences. The close of the poem, where Frost will redefine "singing" for us so as to be able to include the oven bird among the other singers, depends, in part, for its authority on the two falls we have discussed above. One fall is clearly the unsung or less celebrated, the recognition of which is part of this poem's bid for freshness and uniqueness, the other the autumn we all know and fear. Frost does some fast work here. The unsung petal fall is unsung or unrecognized by us because it occurs at a time of near-universal celebration. Our yards are filled with the sweet singers of spring, birds building nests, attracting mates, celebrating territories, and later the hungry cheering of the young. In autumn too we tend not to be able to get the full story; we are, in Frost's words elsewhere, "too absent spirited" to notice. This interlocking of loss as obscured by or distracted by celebration, and a time of lament so pervasive as to obscure the rare singer among us, makes of the poem a bastion of irony. For most of us, who dropped our guards after the announcement of the universal proposition in line 1, such complex irony is so unexpected as to pass not only unchampioned but probably also unnoticed. Among the other structural elements must be reckoned the not-inconsiderable contribution of the meter.

Frost's sonnets generally are richly various in their metrical procedures and rhythmical investigations. All of them pose generally as basic iambic pentameter creations, but in actual development few keep faith with meter. One like "Hyla Brook" is lucky to sustain even a fourth of its lines in any strict form. In fact Frost uses the return to iambic pentameter in the last line, after its long absence, as an ecstatic device. "The Oven Bird" is, in contrast, maddeningly regular. Ignoring little deformations here and there caused by the hyphenated words, the poem is almost perfectly iambic, and nearly perfectly pentameter. Only line 2 interrupts the iambic flow at the start of the line—and in doing so has its own special and urgent reasons. This disruption at the beginning of the line disrupts the rest of the line as well, but line 2 is the only line to do this, whereas in other sonnets there would be many such lines. Line 3's "tree trunks" is also an aberrant spot in the iambic sequence, but it is possible in reading it aloud to force the iambic to conform without violating any reasonable expectation of intonation and inflection. Indeed, all that is rhythmically diverse in the poem occurs in the first three lines where Frost quite typically works hard to catch and engage our attention. Thereafter the movement is as strict and regular as marching. As to syllable count all lines have ten syllables except lines 4 and 7, the flowers/showers rhyme pair, which have eleven. *Flowers* and *showers* thereby become the only two feminine endings in the poem, which help account for how the petal-fall passage are so much more interesting and why the flowers seem beautiful. Otherwise it's all rather relentless, and yet falls short of what might be monotony precisely because the iambic stressing stresses important words. Pear and cherry, one to ten, that other fall we name the fall, "But that he knows in singing not to sing." And so on. Right down to the last lines:

> The question that he frames in all but words
> Is what to make of a diminished thing.

The last line does compromise with the stress of the indefinite article, but the compromise is necessary given the use of "diminished," a somewhat unusual word, and one whose stress is on the middle syllable. The importance of "diminished," its capacity not only to give the one final major interpretation to the bird, and to summarize its behavior as well as its thematic capacity within Frost's work at large, overwhelmingly compensates for any distortion created by elevating the importance of the article. What the resultant regularity of the meter accomplishes is quite obvious but very important. It makes "The Oven Bird" factual and strict. It contributes an atmosphere of reportage—the sort of tone newscasters work very hard to acquire and maintain. This is not the style of argument—it is beyond argument. It is not the style of infatuation or discovery; it is too cool and objective for that. It is more the mode of process itself, a day-by-day, syllable by syllable, opening and closing, the march toward extinction. It does, of course, make the poem seem static and (not to enjoy the pun too much) *wooden*, but it also makes the movement of the poem relentless and inexorable. And it is through this movement that the poem bids to persuade, and, finally, for me, does so.

One might also wish to mention how rich the poem is in little words. A good many of its syllables are contributed by words of no more than two letters—the present tense form of "to be," *is* being notably dominant among them. The net effect of all these declarations and equations is to further fix the propositions toward the implacable. Paucity of polysyllabic words also may be credited to the degree of imaginative energy the poet has, perhaps even the poet's capacity through language to resist or counter the growing domination of mood. There is little resistance. The poet is not, here, as in "Hyla Brook" capable of making an emergency commando rescue mission. Earlier I posited Frost as being present as a component of the "everyone." Thereafter, for the middle of the poem anyway, his role is to take dictation, to write the bird's pronouncements. Only at the end does the poet re-establish the distinction between himself and the bird, but by then he seems nearly congruent with it, totally under its spell.

What is true for "Hyla Brook" and "Mowing" is, however, true for "The Oven Bird." In the closing four or five lines of these sonnets Frost writes lines that seem highly energized or strangely turned. In "Mowing" and "Hyla Brook" these passages I have called tortured or high-density areas. In "The Oven Bird" these lines are 11 and 12—"The bird would cease and be as other birds/ But that it knows in singing not to sing." But here there is no ambition to do anything other than to let the meter take hold and run out, the meter being so consistent within the overall ambition of the poem. And so we have two lines whose meaning may seem a bit obscure but whose rhythm is tamed. The final two lines of the poem, which in "Hyla Brook" and "Mowing," are, in effect, "set up" in the tortured passages, are also, however, set up quite nicely here in that they almost perfectly parallel the preceding two. Each pair of lines is a sentence. And they are almost reversible. Lines 11 and 12 present the contrariness we identify so often as Frost's indomitable spirit—in "Hyla Brook" the poet sings despite the absence of reason to sing. In "The Oven Bird" the bird sings but does not sing a happy song so as not to make light of the diminished world in which he finds himself. These last four lines are inextricably bound—the abab rhyme locks them. They make as strongly-held an ending as we find in the sonnets. So tightly are they interlocked they remind us of the interlocking complementaries discussed earlier. Secure as they are they admit of no contradiction, no ray of hope, no sign of relief, and no look to the future.

Frost is often presented as a nature poet, and frequently linked to notions of cycles of decay and renewal. He deals with cycles often enough. But he does peculiar unlikely things with them. In "Hyla Brook" he refuses to be consoled by what anyone would know will be the return of the brook's song in the melt of the winter snow still yet to come again. In "Spring Pools" he gets himself in a lamenting mood and can't get out of it. No one can tell him to look ahead to when times may be even worse. It is the present loss he knows and suffers. Similarly the mourner in "Spring Pools" will not be reconciled by the stoicism of "The Oven Bird." In Frost's fierce inconsolability in all these poems of lament, however, he honors an important truth for us, that human emotions are not infinitely flexible nor multiply interchangeable. Neither are they reasonable. We live in time and are trapped in time. We will die or someone we love will die. It will happen in the morning, or at close of day, or at the end of some season. Ever after that time will be forever identified with loss. Moreover, the earth in its rhythms and movements offers an annual schooling in the art of giving up and letting go. It is really the same film strip over and over. And if you are astute enough, or melancholy enough, as Frost is here in "The Oven

Bird," you may even find more to cry about.

The most puzzling line of "The Oven Bird" is line 10 in which "the highway dust is over all." This "improves" or rather impairs considerably the "moment overcast" of an earlier line. "A moment overcast" is but a moment, and though it meant the undoing of the petals, we are not such silly creatures as they. But this highway dust is an overcast of a more serious nature. It is "over all." Quite poignantly, it is a pall of our own making, and because it is, it jumps the poem out into a new dimension altogether. Formerly the bird had only natural dissolution and evolution to comment on. Now we have stepped across into the natural world and disturbed its order. Now when the bird speaks, it speaks not only of the sadness of natural decay but of the damage done by man's less than natural acts. Frost is not especially a student of ecology, but his delicate sensibility had already suffered the pain of witnessing human encroachment upon the wilderness. It had suffered doubly in having also to see the failure of human purposes upon a nature that consults only its own laws. There is certainly for us and for the poet enough to be sad about all round. What makes the highway dust so wonderful is that it is so ominous, so much prophetic of that doom we have come, in these past decades, to know well and fear deeply. Even so, in this poem, it is a casual remark. It is but a sort of interlude, a transition, perhaps a little afterthought to balance with the afterthought of the hard-to-remember flowers of line 4. It makes the poem quite modern, however, if it wants to be, if we need it to be. Frost, I think, would like to believe that trees and birds and leaves and flowers are still important enough for us not to need some special framing or apology. They are and they don't. It is poems like "The Oven Bird" that both demonstrate and sustain these living powers.

Robert Frost Restores the Waters to "Hyla Brook"

A brook, our brook, is missing. It has gone the way of all things seasonal. By June its song is gone, as is its speed. We say goodbye. Goodbye "our brook," your song and speed are done. But no, we'll bring it back. But no, we'll go against the orders of the earth, we'll seek it out in unfamiliar zones, and stand upon the very ground it took, and on its own death bed we'll call for it and reason at its loss. And we'll remember it? And play at being naturalists to know the name of what lives in its place. And look for resurrections in the dust. We'll have our brook again or we'll be damned.

> By June our brook's run out of song and speed.
> Sought for much after that, it will be found
> Either to have gone groping underground
> (And taken with it all the Hyla breed
> That shouted in the mist a month ago,
> Like ghost of sleigh-bells in a ghost of snow)—
> Or flourished and come up in jewel-weed,
> Weak foliage that is blown upon and bent
> Even against the way its waters went.
> Its bed is left a faded paper sheet
> Of dead leaves stuck together by the heat—
> A brook to none but who remember long.
> This as it will be seen is other far
> Than with brooks taken otherwhere in song.
> We love the things we love for what they are.

Robert Frost is a poet we should all admire for his courage to throw up contradictions in the face of the inevitable. How many poets are there who have come and gone, do you think, who have moaned away their losses in their verses, or who, resolved toward something good to come, look forward to another year, another place or face in the world's sad comedy. Or begged to be transported through some fantasy to when, a few weeks back, Hyla Brook was lovely in its waters still. Or who insist they take us on a voyage to a neverland where things unchanged, unchanging, live in eternal youth. This is the poetry of fondnesses and forgetfulness. And we have had it all our lives, and to our children bring it for its beauty to console. But Frost knows beauty too. We feel it always in his poems that one eye attends upon the beautiful. But it is not easy with him. Things do not get better with a wish.

Frost's skill is much in evidence in the first line of "Hyla Brook." His assignment, as we have come to know it from reading others of his poems, is to use meter not as some mere technical device of poetry, something which poets have by license or decree, but to show how meter springs out of the physical world, or how meter pays homage to things of the world with similar movements and intervals. In "Mowing," for example, Frost seeks to identify the rhythm of working, of cutting grass with a scythe, with the movement of stresses in his verse lines. The rhythm of work is itself perhaps an art imitative from nature. With the subject here, a brook, Frost is working more closely to original things, how because of gravity and the fact that water is liquid and moves downhill over whatever is in the way it makes a sound which poetry listens to and has sought, perhaps from our first primitive responses, to recreate. Bird song, wind, the sound of rain, the sound of flowing water, the ebb and flow of waves on the shore, thus the earth finds its own voice. Poets have always found kinship with flowing streams, found in the waters confirmation for their singing, and irony—to be carried along by the water in that constant changing and yet to be unchanged. As poet Frost comes late to the scene. Poets have for centuries scavenged the earth for analogies, symbols, signs of wonder, and fabricated toward belief with all kinds of eloquence their songs in tribute and accusation, illusion and disillusion. Things get old, and every day a fading. And yet the seasons turn new again year after year. Much has been made of Frost's inheritance of a diminished New England, and we might ask if it is not this loss in which so many of the poems are steeped. But from what does Frost's contrary spirit come?

Hyla Brook dwindles. Frost remains the same. The natural world is salient in change, and natural change reflects our own fading. Combinations and permutations are multiple. The poet may, on any given day, have lost his love, and comes upon a tree that's lost a branch, a brook that is no more, a bird whose song is somber and dull. Or the poet is full of his own glory and success, only to walk into the shade of trees and find there, losing his way, "a house that is no more a house." Or on another day discover his restlessness matches that of the windy trees outside his window, or that his restlessness takes its origin in that restlessness of the trees. Or in depression be reminded of the joys of life as carried in some dancing happy thing.

"Hyla Brook" is a poem where nature reminds Frost of something but where nature seems not in any position to do anything. It is a poem where the poet is a hero, like so many of Frost's poems, and where language does the keeping. Frost's best work is where the poet takes on almost more than he can handle, where hope of rescue seems remote. This is not to say that very much of consequence happens in Frost's poems. They are heroic nonetheless because they are about what the spirit can absorb without being broken, or, in less severe emotional weathers, the encouragement and discouragement of life, the ups and downs we encounter and the ups and downs we make for ourselves. The survivor metaphor has been very popular in our culture lately. Frost is one of those who might have invented it. His poems are filled with testing how the world tests us, and how we test ourselves against difficulty. Frost's famous competitiveness in life may be the poetic instinct run wild, or the tension the poems are sustained in or invent to resolve are that same testing made tame in art.

Given a brook that sings Frost's metric takes reinforcement through the image. The iambic pentameter line has as its province the carrying through or acting out of the sound the brook makes. Or the potential for this exists. Poems have flow as brooks do. The natural interval in speech between words that seem louder or more assertive and words that are subsidiary or supportive in nature approximates the run of loud and soft one hears in the sound a brook makes. Frost's commitment to iambic poetry then serves him well here in that he has a vehicle which imitates nature: "By June our brook's run out of song and speed." In this first line we hear the brook. We hear it in the flow of the words, in the recurrent loudening and softening of voice. This first line is complex. Rhythmically it recreates the brook in its iambic pentameter. But the sense of the line indicates that the brook is gone. In effect then Frost is withdrawing the brook from us even as he is presenting it. The first line says— here is Hyla Brook—let us listen to it move—while it also says that Hyla Brook has run out. The brook is both present and absent, both coming and going. In a later poem, "The Sound of Trees," Frost explores a similar sound, wind in branches, and tells of how for all their talk of going "they never get away." Part of the task of the first line is to show us the failure of the brook through the iambic meter which carries it and speaks for its presence. And Frost does this beautifully in the slight imperfections he builds into the line. The first is how "our" which should be a less-stressed syllable in the pattern is not securely one syllable and not securely unstressed. "Our" can be two syllables, should you pronounce it that way, and because it is a personal pronoun it gets more attention than if Frost had used merely the definite article. The fourth word "brook's" presents problems also. A simple plural would permit heavy stress, but "brook's" is a contraction of the two words "brook" and "has," and the possibility then exists for the reader to partially voice the absent second syllable—to say "brook" by itself and then the "s" for the missing "has." Already the line has a lot more variation in it than any pure iambic line. But there are other problems. Brooks commonly run, and that is not so unusual, but because the verb "run" follows "brook's" can't give it the natural stress the verb deserves and usually gets. The sixth word, as we get to it, says that we were right to feel that we should assign less stress to "run" because now the verb we discover is not "to run" but "to run out." This allows us a quick restoration of a semblance of the iambic line: stress on *June* and *brook's* and *out*. But Frost has something different to say, and will keep us off balance longer. When we get to the seventh word, "of" we realize that Frost is not picturing a brook that runs out into a larger stream or into a lake but *runs out of* the way we are said to run out of money or patience or time. "Song and speed" are a final problem. They don't want to be separated. They are as if the very substance of the brook, its water. And so tend to adhere to each other, to pair up at the end of the line in a metrical combination of their own. Song and speed in the poems of Robert Frost—love and death in the American novel. But being that they name things which are gone, are absent, they slip from us, resist our bearing down on them, and so the line doesn't firm out in a strict iambic pattern. Taken from the first iambic pair there is a growing loudness to the voice through "our brook's" and "run out" and a gradual lessening toward the end. In the early part of the line we can't predict what Frost's going to tell us. It's possible, even probable, that he's going to assert something positive or bountiful like "By June our brook's a power on the hill." Or "By June our brook's thawed out and come on strong." Instead the message is quite negative—the brook is impoverished, diminished, or to quote from Frost elsewhere—there's "no more to build on there."

What happens when I read the first line is something like this. My voice takes the lead from the opening two syllables to expect iambic security (By June) and goes on into the next words putting them into the pattern that reading the poem thus far and Frost's work at large prepare me for. And I am more or less successful. The line roughly complies with an iambic pentameter formula. At the same time there is a blurring from "our" and "brook's" and the strange sliding of "run " and "run out" and "run out of." Brooks that *run* are vital and strong and taken at their strength. Brooks that "run out" may also be vital in the force they bring to wherever they get to, but there is a degree of weakening here, perhaps the erosive effects of time, a giving way to something else. Brooks that "run out of" song and speed have, presumably little left to offer. And so I have progressed through the line, my prospects diminishing, my outlook becoming more bleak. It is as if I watch the brook that might have been (or once was) diminishing to nothing before my eyes. We are getting it both ways. In the words and in the meter. The meter seems to try to keep firm footing in a pattern of recurrent forcefulness; out it slips and slides and hesitates and fails and forgets itself. We can turn this around though by asking what it is that Frost wishes to emphasize. He has a brook that's run out, and the line runs out and ends with a period. But the poem goes on. And even in the line we can say that the line *runs*, and its last word takes the stress it's supposed to get.

The first line of "Hyla Brook" is almost a poem in itself. It gives us the brook and takes it away. It shows us the brook struggling and dying. In the meter of the line we are made to feel what the brook is in terms of what it was, to sing the song of the brook while also admitting to its loss. This is an altogether brilliant line, as wonderful in its way as the great opening line of "Directive" or the enchanting first line of "Mowing."

What this first line gives us is essential to the poem. The brook is both absent as the poet tells us but is present also for having been selected for discussion. The meter is doing some of the keeping for us, or memory of the brook in its full flowing is manifest in meter. By its very pattern iambic meter places equal emphasis on presence and absence—every stressed syllable a presence, every unstressed an absence. In its sequence beginning with unstressed and rising toward stress (and ending on a stressed syllable) there is a slight emphasis given to the positive; and so the first line for all its skirmishing between the two states comes out a bit more on the encouraging side. But in the meantime the interplay is established, and Frost will continue in the following lines to play off one expectation against another. He will even go so far as to create in "jewel-weed" a term which embodies both, which yokes the two together. (Jewel-weed becomes as important to "Hyla Brook" as "whispering" is to "Mowing.") At the end of line 2, for instance, "it will be found" raises our spirits momentarily, only to have them deflated again in line 3. The brook will be found *to have gone*. And so on. This pattern of rising and falling expectation is central to the poem, and is of course a working out on a large scale of the iambic meter. This play of presence and absence seems central to Frost's work generally, or at least his best poems. It is the source of their wonderful tension. It keeps us interested, on edge, off balance, and makes of the poem a real adventure, something like an athletic contest whose outcome is never clear until the final bell. In "Hyla Brook" the battle hinges on how much Frost will attempt to follow the brook, how much and when he will yield to the fact of its loss, or how he will attempt to bring the brook back. The two instincts, letting go or saving, are reciprocal. Some poems are not able to sustain the struggle for long. In some acceptance occurs off stage, earlier, and we have only the gradual easing into it. In the most dramatic and intense poems the outcome is in doubt nearly throughout. This conflict is Frost's argument with existence, but on a more basic level it may be seen to derive from the essential struggle for poise and meaning in the face of an overwhelming meaninglessness. We gain, we lose, we open to experience, we close down, we risk, we retreat to consolidate, we fight, we flee, we grow stronger, we weaken. This process is extremely compelling. Frost is stretched often to what seem the limits of his resources. At times he seems almost unable to go on. And then he does.

The second line of "Hyla Brook" is not so interesting as the first but it is a strange one too. Its first job is to pick up after line one. The brook is gone, or seems to be. Its absence is beginning to sink in. Frost is allowed a choice here between active or passive voice. His use of "our" sets the precedent for a first person plural, a couple of people going out to look for the brook, a sort of search party. But he chooses instead a passive voice which he then persists in for thirteen more lines, all the way through the official sonnet length, and not changing until he re-establishes the "we" in line fifteen. This delay is quite effective in that a sense of helplessness persists in the poem for a long long time, as if the struggle to regain the brook is taken against huge odds. When Frost does finally in the last line lay claim to the first person plural it is that much more powerful for having been postponed so long. Otherwise line 2 is interesting for its unusual ambiguity. "Sought for much after that," is how it begins. This can be taken two ways. One can seek for the brook much after the beginning of June only to discover that—or one can seek *much* for the brook after the beginning of June. I think Frost makes ambiguity merely for the sake of having it, and at first in this poem the ambiguity seems to no real purpose except that in the second reading we hear a call to those whose commitment is serious. What it amounts to is what he is saying in "Directive"—that those who expect to find this brook, this secret, must be ready to work hard; it is not for everyone. It is not for the idle or lazy. This calling out to those who would be "in on the game" is much more self conscious and explicit in "Directive" (as the title alone implies), and, to my taste is an inferior technique as compared with what we have in "Hyla Brook." In the greater Frost poems he does his work more behind the scenes. Poems like "Mowing" and "The Oven Bird" involve us within their circumstances by creating undeniably compelling situations. What fascinates the poet fascinates us. A certain amount of self-consciousness is always present, however, in a Frost poem. Somewhere along the poet seems to become aware of his audience or aware that he is in fact writing a poem. At its best, say in "The Road Not Taken," we accept this as an expression of Frost's candor. At its worst, perhaps in "New Hampshire," Frost becomes a director intruding on his own drama or movie. Many of Frost's later poems become infected by this self-glorifying pose—probably as a result of his incredible success at barding around. The "I" becomes swollen and self-referential, whereas in the earlier poems the "I" is modest, or merely investigative, a vehicle through which explorations are made and reported. Line 2 begins the give-and-take of absence and presence I mentioned earlier. The line ends with rising meter and rising expectation—that the brook may indeed "be found." Perhaps "song and speed" do not comprise the whole of what the brook has to offer. Perhaps the "that" of "much after that" refers in part to the "song and speed" we can give up on in order to look for other elements. (This is another possibility, admittedly more vague, implicit in line 2.) And so where line 1 ended with the brook gone, line 2 ends with the chance that it may still exist. Starting at this point one can trace quickly through the coming lines. The poet is encouraged at the end of line 2, and line 3 begins with not just one possibility but the two implied by "either." Line 3 then ends disappointingly with "gone groping underground" only to lead us into lines 4, 5, and 6, which are parenthetical. The first of these introduce the Hyla breed, the

Greg Kuzma

frogs that give their name to the brook and poem. They are something we did not know we lost when we lost the brook, and so our sense of loss deepens. They are *all* gone—not one is left. But as Frost goes on to elaborate on the frogs and how they are involved there is a growing sense of richness. They "shouted in the mist a month ago," a line rollicking in its rhythm and pretty in its sounds, gives us the lovely alliteration on "mist" and "month," both stressed syllables separated by the "a." The irony is delightful—that in telling us how much the brook is gone he is bringing it back. In doing this he is also making it more his, by showing how well he has attended to it he is defining it as his own and thus justifying the "our" of the first line. The simile of line 6 further amplifies the sound of frogs while also taking us further back than a month: "Like ghost of sleigh-bells in a ghost of snow." Many critics have remarked the loveliness of this line. Frost takes pleasure in giving us such unexpected bonuses. Now we have the winter we hardly thought to be reminded of. The line also explains the true source of this kind of brook—it arises from winter snows and runs out with the melting. (It's hard to resist comparing it to Frost's famous figure the poem makes—the block of ice on a stove that rides on its own melting.) Later on, when we start looking for how "Hyla Brook" ends up one line too long we should have kept this line in mind—it is an unexpected flourish in a poem that has been otherwise rather matter-of-fact. At this point, though, it is important to note that the "groping underground" passage has produced some astonishing results. Instead of a blind wounded thing Frost gives us shouting and mist and sleigh-bells. This then makes the supposed contrast between "groping underground" and the "flourished" of line 7 not nearly the contrast it might have been. In fact the contrast dissolves. So when Frost gets to "flourished" in line 7 he's already established a flourish for us. How this translates back in terms of our pattern is that line 3, which seemed to end discouragingly, opens on a passage where the brook thrives. Absence becomes presence, and if we are to continue in this same mode, presence (the *flourished* of line 8) should become absence. And it does. The "jewel-weed" is *weak*.

Jewel-weed is an exciting prospect. The name and its role seem to have been designed precisely by a poet so inclined as Frost is who wishes to make the most of things as they are. The brook is gone, but, by some law of compensation, leaves in its wake, in its bed, the "jewel" by which we may remember the sparkling waters. (Not only is the countryside abundant with metaphoric delight but so also the language itself, the given names of things.) "Jewel-weed" is doubly blessed. "Jewel" recalls the splendor of the jewel-like brook when it is full and dazzling over the rocks, while "weed" implies the ugliness of its diminished condition. So perfect is the word for Frost here as a symbol for the problem at hand that we might suspect he coined it—he did not. And "jewel-weed" is even richer than we have said so far, for in its "weed" it offers the promise of strength and hardiness, qualities the poet should welcome at this point. If there is no more water we may then have plants to contain it—plants that sparkle like jewels but that are also long-enduring. Certainly they will keep the faith, keep true to the brook. But as our spirits are raised in this compound evocativeness of the name of the plant, they are shattered immediately upon the start of the next line. Frost now does a neat thing! He takes the "we" of weed and builds the new word "weak." He borrows from a word that ought to be hardy enough to lend a bit of itself without harm, but in the process destroys it. Where repetition of the "we" helps bind the poem together over the interval of lines, when Frost makes a word out of the "we" the word he makes contradicts a main sense of "weeds"—that they are hardy tenacious things. No, he says, they're "Weak"! Or their foliage is, whatever that means. "Foliage" itself may disappoint after "jewel"—and further confound the paradox. Foliage picks up strength as a word from "flourish" by parallel positioning, but foliage is not where we would expect to see the sparkling jewels of the lost waters. Wasn't it flowers in their brilliant colors or crystalline shapes we expected? But there are no flowers; there is nothing but foliage, and weak foliage at that.

Frost's capacity to tune our ears in close harmony with his music is one of his strengths. Any poem that works for us as a self-contained thing coordinates its sounds in such a way that after a while the family of sounds becomes selective from whatever prospective sounds are needed. From the side of sound the poem may become easier to write even at the same time that the sense of the poem may force us to choose from a narrowing range of possibilities.

What I'm saying is sound is the more free component; that among the many words that rhyme with "song" for instance, Frost has a shorter list of words that work within his purposes. Sounds lead, and meanings catch up. Feeling is first, as Cummings says. The senses first, and then the sense, or the pressure we put on sense. But sounds may force meanings. A sound the poet is attracted to just won't let him go—and he may end up using it many times. One of the problems we need to examine in "Hyla Brook" is where the last line comes from, and how it is that Frost so boldly and so successfully concludes the poem with such an acute and active line. Or where the "we" comes from! Certainly it comes from "our" in the first line, but fourteen lines is a rather long interval over which to wait. Frost's play then on the "we" he isolates from "weed" and transports into "weak" provides a halfway relay for the energy. The last line can still be surprising, a sudden leap, but it must also be seen to grow out of the rest of the poem. Midway through the poet establishes the "we" and keeps it alive in the coming lines in such words as "went" and "sheet" and "heat" and "remember" and "will" and "with" and "otherwhere."

Frost goes right into line 8 with its "Weak foliage" as if this is what we expect. But that's typical of Frost. He says the strangest things and seems not the least surprised. Why should a flourish be weak, in any sense? And yet the poem rolls right along under the obligation it has made to tell us where the brook has gone. It almost seems determined to do so, and sets its jaw against whatever unhappy thing it discovers in the process. Or we can say what we said earlier—that which marks the going underground toward absence produces the memory in which the brook thrives, and so that which presumably depicts flourishing ought to show diminishment. The jewel-weed is weak in that it blows about in the wind "even against the way its waters went." (We will need to explore later the implications of this within the large ambition of the poem.) But the movement of these lines shows no hesitancy or faltering or sadness—the lines move with great dispatch as if they were telling us happier things. The assonance of "against" and "went" is a contributing factor, but alliteration with "blown upon and bent" is also contributing. And then we have more alliteration in "way its waters went." One almost might suppose that Frost forgets that he is supposed to be disappointed. Instead of a tone of regret or grief the lines are lively and full of the energy of things going off to somewhere exciting. These high spirits are not really deserved, unless, of course, one has given up effecting to find the brook in any real sense. I think this is the case. Frost really does say goodbye to the brook as we know it in line 1-- and no natural transformation of it or evolution of it is satisfactory. But the high spirits of this line can be traced back to the parenthetical passage earlier. There the lines are ecstatic with sleighbells and snow and the repetition of "ghost." Ghost alliterates on itself, rhymes itself. So that the alliteration we are now in is indebted to how unquestioning we were in line 6. One could add, though, that the "b"words in line eight have their own reason for seeming natural. When we blow upon something we expect something to happen as a reaction—that is how things are in our physical universe. Or we can go all the way back to lullabies from childhood— when the wind blows the bough bends. How many times we fell asleep to this cadence! In line 9 Frost pushes the natural inevitability of things further by alliterating on three words— "way" and "waters" and "went." How properly in harmony these words sound! How can anything be wrong when the sounds are so right. So at the end of line 9 we find the poet strangely in accord with things as they are. The wind blows and the jewel-weed bends. More important, Frost's acceptance of the way things are with the brook even as the jewel-weed cannot keep the current prepares us for the explicit statement of acceptance made in the last line.

What I've been analyzing for so long is the second sentence of "Hyla Brook." The second sentence is really an elaboration of the first. It is also a rehearsal of the mood of the first but with elaboration backwards in time as well as an extremely sensitive depiction of the brook's present situation. Altogether it makes for a degree of exhaustiveness not felt earlier. Frost tries to show the brook going and staying and struggling to stay, all in the first line, and all exclusively in terms of the meter. In the second sentence the same battle is waged, but Frost uses much more the full range of poetry's resources. Yet even this more total commitment does not save the brook. I think we can feel to what extent Frost is exhausted in the tenth line: "Its bed is left a faded paper sheet." The set jaw speaks, through thin lips. All the joy of exclaiming went off with the waters. This voice is depleted of possibility, a thin dry voice through clenched teeth. Lines 8 and 9 have shown Frost being swept along. They act out in more immediate and vibrant terms what the play in the first sentence had merely sketched. They make a restoration of the running out. But now there is an added dimension. Line 9 carries two movements in it—the blowing of the jewel-weed backwards against the current and the current itself, the "way the waters went." The foliage is, as Frost says, weak, not steadfast nor tenacious nor loyal nor hardy. It has betrayed the way of the waters, and not only in slight deviations from "the way" but in absolute contradiction to it, in precise opposition. In "West Running Brook" Frost will make a great insight into existence in this "backward motion toward the source" he sees in the curl of the white wave. Things are not so clarified or developed here in "Hyla Brook," but the situation is just as complex and the more obscure for being almost entirely implicit. Jewel-weed disappoints because it will not hold true to the memory of the current, but at the same time it does resist the brook's leaving. Two instincts contend in the lines, inhabit, in fact, the same words, and these contrary instincts cannot contend forever. In lines 8 and 9, Frost is surrendering. Now, at last, he turns his eye upon the "faded" bed of the brook, and in a voice diminished to something both mechanical and barely audible he feels his way along syllable by syllable in line 10. This line may not be Frost's absolutely bleakest line, but it surely is one of them. Everything that can be done has been done. All hope is lost.

The voice is sustained merely by habit alone; the rhythm is a meter stiff and lifeless. The sounds of the words are without roundness or color— "is" is "its" without the "t," "bed" and "left" have to share the same sounds, as if Frost has exhausted his vocabulary, and "faded" and "paper" rhyme on their first syllables but not their second. Little of the shaping and binding instincts remain. This is a voice bereft. Taken in sequence, reading the line, one cannot help but feel Frost is making the line up in its sounds out of the ashes or shattered bodies of the words as he uses them and uses them up. There is the undeniable sense of diminishment, loss, things reduced to the barest essentials, that life holds out here but just barely. Line 11 adds to this feeling of woe by rhyming "dead" on "bed" in position two of line 10, and in its depressing image of "dead leaves stuck together by the heat." And how it ends—with the dash—as if Frost just can't go any further— that he is emotionally drained—that there is nothing left to say.

The word "sheet" at the end of line 10 is a rather bright sound even as in its image it cooperates with the mood. As an end word in a rhymed poem it anticipates its rhyme partner. When Frost rhymes it with the phrase "stuck together by the heat" he cancels out most of its brightness. But are we not surprised that we can still be disappointed? Are we still looking for even a glimmer of hope? Or is the form of the poem itself a consolation to us with its matching and pairing and rhyming, with no thing alone without some complement. Somewhere in this part of the poem readers invariably remark that they begin to think of rescue by poetry. How, if all else fails, we can always write a poem about it. One critic points out that "paper sheet" is just the thing for poets to write a poem on. And Frost too turns toward poetry, to "song," which has been synonymous with poetry down through history. Line 12 at first seems rather forgettable—"A brook to none but who remember long." It does little more than keep the poem moving. It does, however, begin to make room for a degree of self consciousness we have not had. It is no brook unless it is to someone who remembers. In context it is saying "I am one who remembers long." It says the brook exists as it does here in this telling because "I am special in my way."

The transition from a speaker who is not self-conscious, one concerned with the relationship between himself and the brook, and nothing else, to the different speaker we now find is an important development in this poem. Somewhere in lines 10, 11, and 12 Frost begins his movement outward beyond the confines of the dramatic situation. But maybe dramatic situation in this poem has never been as clear-cut or predictable as we would want. There was a degree of intimacy at the very start—"our brook"—as if we partake with him of some agreement. We agree to be a part of the "we" just enough so that what the famous poet is going to make of all this is something we agree to watch and care for. The poem becomes a magic show with Frost as magician and ourselves as both audience and apprentices.

Lines 13 and 14 are among the strangest in any Frost poem. They have an awkwardness about them which is hard to get over or forgive. They seem strained and labored, the desperate reaching of someone nearly at the limits of what he can do. For many readers, I expect, they flaw the poem seriously. "Hyla Brook" is rarely discussed in essays on Frost's work, and has been left out of the Rinehart edition of the selected poems. But to me these lines make the poem more daring and audacious—without them I don't think Frost would have discovered the truth of the last line—or without them the last line would not seem so brilliantly correct. But where do the lines come from?—how do we justify them? Are they proof of Frost's arrogance; do they indicate to what lengths Frost will go, *even in his poems*, to make himself seem the exception in all things? Or are they honest; the poet having taken the impulse far enough to the point of some new awareness and recognition? Are they not the inevitable result of loss and how it affects us—when, having done all we can for ourselves, we turn outward to others, to history, to tradition? The brook is gone and Frost has paid his respects. He has even tried to see through its present circumstance to recall it as it once was—and in so doing he has made it sing again in his various images. But he has pushed to the length of his inventiveness, and he has endured its diminished state as much as could be expected. And now he turns to us to remind us, ere we fault him for his failure, that ours is a rather unique situation. Poets don't celebrate lost brooks, brooks that have lost their song and speed. And if we can't recall that this is the case he will give us time in the future to reflect upon it—this "as it will be seen" he writes. And so let us please then pardon him for his extraordinary efforts.

The lameness of these lines may be attributed to Frost the writer who, toward the end of his otherwise normal sonnet, discovers he doesn't have sufficient room to say what he needs to say in the provided space remaining and so must bunch things up rather awkwardly. Or the artificial poetic sound of the lines may be partly a corruption visited upon Frost's language as it attempts to contemplate the "other far" of traditional poetry. That art being so unnatural as to deform Frost's otherwise normal language as it moves in contemplation of it. "Other far" and "otherwhere" are pretty bad, however we want to try to justify them, but they are better together than they would be alone. Or having said "other far" and gotten away with it "otherwhere" has a precedent to stand on. Or the two can keep each other company. Frost often tries to bluff out such problem passages. He'll say again what he should be trying to find a way to apologize for. Or in saying something close in its diction to what he's said already he begins to assimilate it toward naturalness, begins to take some of the strangeness out of it. On the level of sound alone Frost has prepared the way for these phrases in the earlier lines. Lines 9, 10, 11, and 12, employ "other" type words in parallel positions. Line 9 has "waters" second from the end, and the others have "paper" and "together" and "remember" respectively. There is a little colony of such related creatures towards the ends of these lines. And so "other far" and "otherwhere" are not so odd in sound although they are unnatural in diction. Of the two "other far" is more odd because "otherwhere" reminds us of the more obvious words "elsewheres" or "somewhere" or "somewheres else." But otherwhere is saved a bit by not ending the line—its line ends with "in song," a more normal phrasing. "Other far" has to hang there a bit in the midst of things until Frost satisfies the rhyme with line 15.

Lines 13 and 14 are the strange tortured passage of "Hyla Brook," but Frost's sonnets generally have such passages toward their closings. In "Mowing" Frost writes: "Not without feeble-pointed spikes of flowers/(Pale orchises) and scared a bright green snake." And "The Oven Bird" says in lines eleven and twelve: "The bird would cease and be as other birds/ But that it knows in singing not to sing," surely the most difficult lines of that poem. Such passages are knots of twisted energy in poems otherwise more relaxed. They contrast sharply with the writing which precedes them, giving us an index to how relaxed and casual Frost usually is. In this poem we have the added dimension of the awkwardness as being associated with a more poetic poetry. In all of the sonnets, however, Frost gives us a chance to recover from such language, to escape from it back into a language more natural to what we have been experiencing. It is as if such tortured passages disorient us just enough so that we rush eagerly into the line or lines that follow considerably more inclined to welcome them in whatever ways we can. These passages do incline us to say, however, that Frost is not so comfortable in the sonnet as some others are, but what is far more interesting to note is how Frost puts even this discomfort to work on his behalf. His discomfort becomes ours, and in "Hyla Brook" the difficult lines are a springboard into the airy regions beyond the sonnet. In "Mowing" and "The Oven Bird," in contrast, the difficult passages do not flood into the fourteenth line—Frost gives himself a last bit of room to recover. But here, in order to escape from them, we must plunge beyond the normal body of the sonnet into line fifteen. And do so willingly.

Lines 12, 13, and 14 are sorts of the diversionary moves out sideways Frost is famous for. He admires the curved straightness of a walking stick, or the way an ax helve conforms to the natural bends of the grain in the wood. His poems are filled with oblique movements. The poems *look* logical in overall layout and design, and seem to proceed line by line in logical argument, toward inevitable conclusions, but most of the fun resides in Frost's tangents. "Hyla Brook" has, earlier, that one famous parenthetical section which delivers both frogs and sleighbells, but it might be said that the whole poem, after the first line, is a series of asides which derive emotionally from trying to escape the consequences of admitting the loss of the brook. One thinks of "Out, Out" with its well-known passage "No more to build on there" and the sudden and cruel ending soon after. These asides may also be viewed as that technique by which, faced with the inevitable, we put off accepting it for as long as possible.

The last line of "Hyla Brook" is one of the most remarkable lines in all of Frost's poetry. It both belongs by itself, as its own marvelous encoding, while it also stands as the wondrous culmination of this already dazzling poem. It is simultaneously both a moral to the poem, the poem's inevitable conclusion (if poems are supposed to be so arranged) and an organic part of it which speaks in and of the voice of the poem. It has a rightness compounded of many instincts—it says one last goodbye even as it saves the brook forever, holding it beautifully in its strong and sure meter. Of all Frost's most lovely lines it is the most free, the most original and inspirational and the most bound, the most linked and held by the poem out of which it leaps and in whose voice it speaks in "whole again beyond confusion." As a living organ of the poem it takes its life in many countless bonds of thought and necessity. First Frost needs, plainly, a rhyme for "far." Back at the halfway point in the sonnet he allowed the "jewel-weed" to turn his ear, or he wanted to link the poem all the way back to its original end sound, and thereby created the odd third rhyme. Either he was going to do himself one better and seek a fourth word to rhyme on the "eed" sound, or having a triplet among couplets would have forced him one line short or one line long, a sonnet at thirteen lines or fifteen. Rhymes on "sheet" and "heat" satisfy the option of sustaining the "speed" rhymes, and maybe distract us too, entangle us in a mix of like sounds so we lose "all measure of pace and fixity." Actually Frost carries the "e" sound through every fourth line starting with the first—it ends line 4, line 7, then line 10 and 11. In a conventional sonnet the "e" rhyme would have essentially controlled the poem for eleven out of fourteen lines. By pushing out to fifteen or being drawn out Frost has a whole four-line stanza or section at the end of the poem in which to establish other sounds. What he makes then, really, is a new division for the sonnet, an opening octet increased (on behalf of the struggle which overflows its normal boundaries) to eleven lines, and a concluding quatrain. Another way to divide the poem up more easily is to see it as a series of five tercets whose opening sections are interlocked nicely by delayed rhymes. This looks neat and orderly for three stanzas:

> By June our brook's run out of song and *speed*
> Sought for much after that, it will be *found*
> Either to have gone groping under*ground*
>
> (And taken with it all the Hyla *breed*
> That shouted in the mist a month *ago*,
> Like ghost of sleighbells in a ghost of *snow*)—
>
> Or flourished and come up in jewel-*weed*,
> Weak foliage that is blown upon and *bent*
> Even against the way its waters *went*.

The final two stanzas are acceptable variations of possible solutions. Stanza four inverts the pattern, giving the couplet first and then the lone sound.

> Its bed is left a faded paper *sheet*
> Of dead leaves stuck together by the *heat*—
> A brook to none but who remember *long*.

Stanza five scrambles around to get locked down;

> This, as it will be seen is other far
> Than with brooks taken otherwhere in song.
> We love the things we love for what they are.

To account for "far" we need to recall Frost's instinct toward going outside the scene and the large pressure we are under in these latter lines. It's a credit to Frost, actually, for working the last lines out so intricately when he might just as well have done something like making a triplet on one sound at the end. Finally there's no acceptable way to account for the extra line in any technical way. Precedents exist for tag lines for sonnets for hundreds of years, but Frost is essentially breaking new ground for the modern reader. The main thing is that though the fifteen line sonnet is a technical achievement its impetus springs from emotional sources; we are carried up and along by the poem, uncaring if it turns out right.

Secondly, Frost uses a construction in line 13 which takes us backward in the poem as well as forward. "As it will be seen" recalls for us "it will be found" from line 2, and so makes for a nice balance. The problem with line 13 is that if we take the lead from line 2 we will be now, late in the poem, expecting some considerable exposition. "It will be found," after all, concluded line 1 of a sentence which went on for eight more lines while Frost searched exhaustively for the missing brook. Frost deftly realigns us under the old regime, even as he is preparing to satisfy us not with an exhaustive looking but with a statement in which our "happiness makes up in height for what it lacks in length." But the expression itself contains within it its own future looking. The figurative meaning involves things like "upon reflection" or "you will see if you think about it," or "you will come to realize," while literally thrusting us forward into what space and time we have left *within* the poem. Anything said in a poem has a life of its own and may be detached from it or taken out of context. That is perhaps one of the dangers of writing poetry—you may get remembered not for books or complete poems but for a line here or there. A poem like "Mowing" affords a couple memorable lines one almost wishes to forget the rest of the poem for. In fact, from "Mending Wall" to "Birches" to "Stopping by Woods" to "Directive" Frost is loaded with one liners. More to the point, at any moment in any poem we are, as readers, both in and out of it. We may remark, to ourselves, the felicity of some expression or some phrase that seems especially well turned. Here in "Hyla Brook" Frost takes advantage of that reality by acknowledging our otherness—by giving the otherness, the other far and otherwhere, credibility—and he takes us there for a brief moment before bringing us back within the special time and place of the poem. "That would be good both going and coming back." Which may be one of the otherwheres we go to in this digression. We read one poem in order to read another, he tells us some other place. What is so brilliant about "Hyla Brook" is that Frost goes out of his way to wrench us forcibly out of the safe confines of the poem in order that more pressure be put upon him when he brings us back into it, and that his triumph, if it be so, be the more triumphant. The fact is that the last line of "Hyla Brook" must live to endure in other times and weathers beyond that of the poet and his brook. And so the expression "as it will be seen" may be seen as what it is, a large risk-taking in which all may be lost but everything is also to win.

There are other justifications for line 15. The tortured passage of lines 13 and 14 turn us to the following line where we may regain our stability or equilibrium. The even iambic meter of line 15 does just this. Or we may invoke the famous humility of the poet—if nature be imperfect, if jewel-weed can fail to keep the current, the poet may then fail to execute the sonnet. Imperfect worlds engender imperfect poems— or that is the rationale for this one. Frost may have had another option. He might have ended the poem on line 12, where memory is emphasized—"a brook to none but who remember long." The problem with this, however, is that Frost has not made the brook exist for us only as it *was* for him but as it *is*. Memory alone is not enough—we need how the brook exists to our senses. Line 12 does a good job of summarizing those episodes in the poem that are recalled— frogs and sleighbells—but something else accounts for the brook in its present condition.

Another defense for the last line hinges on how we step outside the poem into the world of other poetry. There Frost tells us we should see how other brooks are presented. The poems which he points us to, even if we do not know them by name or author, must be those which make large statements about experience. "Taken otherwhere" refers, then, both to how brooks become poems and how these poems present an idealized or poetic view of reality. And so if brooks elsewheres in poetry are misrepresented let us for once take them honestly, "for what they are." There's another dimension to this. After reminding us of his forebears, English poets mostly, Frost comes under heavy pressure. Will he defer? Will he defend America's honor? Will he be modest or defensive? No. What he does is attack boldly. He says "I am different. I dare write a fifteen-line sonnet!"

It's hard to know where Frost's supreme self-awareness ends. If he is conscious of himself as poet among other poets he may just as easily be conscious of himself in relation to his own work, what sort of poet he is, what he is likely to do. Having stepped outside the circumstances of the poem, or through them, Frost may become aware of his own inclinations and predilections. He's a wisdom poet, one occasioned to find truth in homely settings like this one, and so he complies, for all the unsophisticated ones, for all those sentimental instincts even cynics sometimes have—he will set down the oracle, "something we can learn by heart and when alone repeat." Another defense, related here, is that Frost takes something admittedly a cliché, or which sounds like one, and attempts to show how such things come into being—the pressures that lead to them, the circumstances of both life and language out of which such statements arise. Clichés are clichés, but once they held the human truth, and lived in faithful keeping to our predicament. We may come late upon the scene, where our language has been with itself so long it has grown stale and awkward and hesitant as to its best purposes, very much indeed like Hyla Brook past June. Somewhere then in the course of the search for the brook Frost finds not its waters but the current of our language and follows it back toward its source. The poem then seeks out something fresh and original in *language*, back in a time of first sayings. And so the last line of the poem seems so vigorous and fresh.

Long long ago the poet went up the mountain looking for Hyla Brook. But it was gone. So in his voice he sang the tune of its going and its going out. And sang it for us in a current of his own, the words of his own mouth, capturing it, holding it gently, letting it rush itself along into oblivion. And spent a good part of a day talking it back, looking here and there for it, and asking how it is or is not there. The pure clean clear iambic of line 15 is the great wonder of this line, and in a line which is the great ecstatic wonder of this poem. Where once, in the first line, the flow of the brook was hesitant and faulty, full of skirmish and skittish and failing energy, in line 15 the song of the brook is sure and firm once more. So the lost waters of Hyla Brook are restored.

A Good Ear—
Charting the Music of
"A Young Birch"

"A Young Birch" is one of Frost's richest poems. Many readers overlook it because its thematic ambition is rather small. It does not involve itself with finding one's way along the road of life, nor is it a poem about loss and what to make of it, nor is it one of the famous monologues or dialogs through which character is discovered and voice becomes so interesting. This is Frost talking, the man who happens to live in the country, the poet at ease, home for a change, back from one of his reading tours, and paying a little homage to some gentle innocent thing whose incidental beauty sustains him on the long way. Perhaps the biggest interference to its being taken seriously is that it "dares to lean,/ Relying" for its subject on a subject already made dazzlingly resonant in the great poem "Birches." "A Young Birch" struggles for identity, autonomy, and a little self respect in the presence of the masterpiece. It is in its shadow, or its small delicate light is all but lost in the greater seeming brilliance of the larger poem.

Perhaps the fate of the poem is pretty much like the fate of the tree, as Frost tells us, to be lucky at all to be spared "from the number of the slain," and to grow, more or less in neglect, in obscurity, "At first to be no bigger than a cane,/ And then no bigger than a fishing pole," and even in its final triumph to be all but dismissed in Frost's recognition of its limits in the word "ornament." This is not one of Frost's great almost totemic trees. Its great dark crown does not spread gloom where its shade falls. A forest does not spring up around it to become life's "pathless wood." Nor is it witness tree. Nor does the wind in it inspire restlessness, the poet off to somewhere, having made the reckless choice. Nor do its roots, in drawing water up, "blot out and drink up and sweep away" the "flowery waters and these watery flowers" in such a fragile world as that of "Spring Pools." The tree is but an *ornament*, and we are to think of nursery stock, perhaps a little puttering around the yard, perhaps the modest pleasure of making things a bit neat and orderly, pulling weeds, the work we do of a Sunday afternoon to ease us off a bit from the real work—making sense of the world, teaching, getting and spending, reading books, giving lectures, writing poems.

Even if Frost had wanted to, and there is some small

evidence he started to try to make of the whiteness of the tree that which he makes of say the whiteness of the quartz, or what Melville makes of the whiteness of the whale, birch trees just won't sustain such heavy bearing. That's what he talks about in "Birches," isn't it?—limbering up in their limbs, limbering their limbs up for a wild ride "To Earthward." There is some serious play with whiteness in the wonderful poem "The Onset." And there is the scary stuff he does with all that *too much* whiteness of spider and flower and moth in "Design." Surely "A Young Birch" is mildly important as one of the poems of whiteness, but just a quick check of the others on the list shows how much more ambitious Frost is in these others. Rather than try to tip the poem toward some advantage it doesn't have, better to take a photograph of this little tree for one of those charming New England calendars.

I don't mean my introduction to be misleading. My opinion of the poem is very different. I only offer these perspectives because I think that they are the usual ones. "A Young Birch," while it may suffer in comparison with many of Frost's greatest poems, is itself a masterpiece though of a different kind. It is intricately, beautifully made, possessed of a gorgeous music. So lovely is it in its sounds, so rich, that it rivals music in its capacity to move us without our really knowing why, its words so much less involved with delivering meanings to our minds than flourishing on our tongues and in our ears. All grace is its, all manner of loveliness.

But this intricacy and complexity I speak of is deceptive, hard to see. A cursory reading of the poem—which is all it usually gets, consigned as it is to minor status—does pick up some of the more obvious play with words. A little alliteration, some assonance and consonance, and of course the rhymes, which, so typical of Frost generally, we find it easy to take for granted. There does seem to be, admittedly, a firmness, a sureness to its movement. It does not seem confused as to what it's saying or going to say, but moves along confidently, befitting, we then may venture, a subject that does not inspire or require hard thought or soul searching. The very proficiency of its technique then is cited to its discredit. The poem has an ease about it, a relaxed quality, a certain lightness, a sense of

Greg Kuzma

engagement, a subject assessed and worked through, a certain thoroughness which Frost achieves in dozens of poems, and even the little wink across the room, poet to audience, with the small joke on the hired help, who just might, with any luck, blunder along and somehow not cut the tree down when our backs are turned while the poet is here educatin' us into the greater mysteries. Nobody makes jokes on Silas—this hired help is not that hired man. It's the same joke we get again and again in Frost—on newspaper types for misquoting him, or not fully quoting him, or proofreaders for thinking he meant "The Sound of *the* Trees." No. Certainly not! "The Sound of Trees." Let's have it that way. Humours of such embarrassments aside, "A Young Birch" is competent, rather clear in its descriptions, if not vivid, pleasantly well crafted, and, like so many Frost poems, ends no further along toward wisdom than it started, though sustained in its capacity to delight.

> The birch begins to crack its outer sheath
> Of baby green and show the white beneath,
> As whosoever likes the young and slight
> May well have noticed. Soon entirely white
> To double day and cut in half the dark
> It will stand forth, entirely white in bark,
> And nothing but the top a leafy green—
> The only native tree that dares to lean,
> Relying on its beauty, to the air.
> (Less brave perhaps than trusting are the fair.)
> And someone reminiscent will recall
> How once in cutting brush along the wall
> He spared it from the number of the slain,
> At first to be no bigger than a cane,
> And then no bigger than a fishing pole,
> But now at last so obvious a bole
> The most efficient help you ever hired
> Would know that it was there to be admired,
> And zeal would not be thanked that cut it down
> When you were reading books or out of town.
> It was a thing of beauty and was sent
> To live its life out as an ornament.

Copying the poem over here, typing it out, I discover again what I learned within a few months of first encountering the poem, than I know it almost by heart. I knew most of it then; I know it even better now. Randall Jarrell talks about his discovering the same thing about other Frost poems, "Provide, Provide," for one, in his still-startling essay "To the Laodiceans." "Stopping by Woods" was quick to learn, but, unlike Jarrell, I had to practice "Provide, Provide" for a week or so before I mastered it. All those gaps between the stanzas are not always the same transitional interval—I found myself thinking I had left things out.

Memorability is one of Frost's strongest qualities, and maybe the chief reason his poems caught on so well with so many people. They gave them something they could "learn/ By heart and when alone repeat." But "A Young Birch" was for me a special case. I picked it up almost at a glance. No, I also heard it read—Frost read it, on a record. Maybe that clinched it. Within a very short time, and without my willing it, whole sections of the poem had become indelible. So when I started teaching Frost occasionally a few years later I put it to myself to try to make time, toward the end of that first course, after we had wrestled with some bigger poems, to try to find out why this poem was so seductive. What follows here is what I've come to understand. It is not a gripping story, in any way. It comes from having been puzzled and yet convinced at the same time that there is indeed something to find.

The work I did that first year and thereafter was modestly successful. Every time I looked at the poem anew I found another little thing I hadn't noticed before. It was like the annual walk over plowed ground at the old Indian encampment—spring thaw was sure to turn up a few new artifacts. It was not until after many years of this sort of lazy picking, and being satisfied with what I found, and my students being satisfied, that there occurred to me a sudden and overwhelming revelation—the supply I picked from, expecting every year that it would some day eventually run out, was, in fact, inexhaustible. In the following pages, I want to suggest some of this small infinity for you.

Scattered amongst these pages are a number of charts. I

wanted not to have to use charts because they seem strained and stiff as well as overly scientific. After all, we're talking about a poem. But the sheer extent of the data forces me to do so. The charts are not in any special sequence. I could not think of any way to order them. There does not seem to be a progression from obvious things toward more and more subtle things, as I had wished there would be.

The dynamic reality of this poem is quite different from that—everything and anything in it is useful in itself, contributory toward some larger effect, and complementary with other similar elements. Nothing is idle or wasted, nothing inessential. Were I to risk an analogy between the poem and the human body, you might think you could find some syllable, a preposition maybe, that is the appendix of this body, or the tonsils, but I have not yet found it. If I had, I would have been quick to remove it, to make the mass of this body less. My first chart is a crude affair. I note only the most obvious features of the poem's sound, the immediate play with the "b" sounds in the first two lines (which also includes "g" in "birch begins" and "baby green"), the "sh" of "sheath" and "show," but also the other strong sound of "sheath"—the "th" sound it ends with and which ends "beneath" in the couplet. (I ignore, for the time being, the question about how involved the "th" of the definite article may be.) Then there's assonance with the long "i" sound. I mark "likes" in line three and then the rhyme pair of "slight" and "white."

This cursory survey omits "white" in line two because I'm already moved on too far to go back. This first chart is of localisms—it presumes a short-term memory—it can look at only fifteen or twenty syllables at a time. It notes the double "d" of "double day," the repetition of initial "n" sounds in "nothing" and "native" because of parallel proximity in consecutive lines, and it gets caught up in the rather subtle transformation of "one" into "scent" into "once" in lines 11 and 12, but it fails to record reiterations and repetitions of intervals over five or six lines, and so leaves unremarked the "reminiscent"/ "efficient"/ "ornament" triad. The inability to work over intervals of five or seven or even ten lines is not necessarily something we should be ashamed of. What prior experience with Frost poems demands such work? Little. A poem like "Mowing" plays with the sound of the scythe but only at the beginning; we are conscious of sound briefly, and then sounds take a subordinate role as Frost's investigation into meaning takes foreground.

Critics develop long term sensitivities almost exclusively on behalf of thematic concerns. Or where metaphor is involved. We expect metaphor to extend the reach of the literal, to create wonderful parallels, often to envelop the whole poem. Imagery is another area where the critic sorts through the whole text. I once saw a paper devoted to water imagery in Sylvia Plath where all the water in all the poems in a whole book was impounded, fenced off and dammed up. Where the poem does have a large musical dimension, too readily will the critic conclude that the musical dimension emasculates the intellectual component, or is distractedly subordinate to it. Vachel Lindsay is not a poet so

Chart 1

The <u>birch</u> <u>begins</u> to crack its outer shea<u>th</u>
Of <u>baby</u> <u>green</u> and show <u>the</u> wh<u>i</u>te benea<u>th</u>,
As whosoever l<u>i</u>kes the young and sl<u>i</u>ght
May well have noticed. Soon entirely wh<u>i</u>te
To <u>d</u>ouble <u>d</u>ay and cut in half the <u>d</u>ark
It will stand <u>f</u>orth, entirely white in bark,
And <u>n</u>othing but the top a lea<u>fy</u> green—
The only <u>n</u>ative tree that dares to lean,
Relying on its <u>b</u>eauty, to the air.
(Less brave perhaps than trusting are the fair.)
And some<u>one</u> remini<u>scent</u> will recall
How <u>once</u> in cutting brush along the wall
He spared it from the number of the slain,
At first to be <u>no bigger than</u> a cane,
And then <u>no bigger than</u> a fishing pole,
But now at last so obvious a bole
The most efficient help you ever hired
Would know <u>th</u>at it was <u>th</u>ere to be admired,
And zeal would not be <u>th</u>anked that <u>cut it down</u>
When you were reading books or <u>out of town</u>.

> It was a <u>thing</u> of beauty and was sent
> To live its life out as an ornament˙

much as a musician of words. Even Dylan Thomas's work gets the brush-off—his lush language too often identified as the fuzzy thinking and thick tongue booze wrought.

My chart tries to show groupings of sound-words throughout the poem, beginning to end, but this is not very compelling. It amounts to forty minutes in class with all of us circling letters and underlining phrases. And when we have done it, "what good" have we done? A few years went by after my initial investigations. I was doing the Frost class nearly every fall. Sometimes we'd work on "A Young Birch" a little, and I'd go over the poem again to pick up some new stuff. One year I got interested in the relationship between "b " and "p" in "bigger than a fishing pole /But now at last so obvious a bole," but soon gave it up as a false issue. One time I noticed a whole sequence of "er" words, that ran from the first line nearly to the end, made some notes about it, but then couldn't find the notes when I went to look for them and only remembered later. Mostly I didn't talk about the poem at all, except in my introductory remarks about where the course might go, time permitting. I began the habit of holding out the "sound poems" as a special unit where, the hard work of puzzling out meanings behind us, we could luxuriate in Frost's beautiful language, a sort of retirement to a life of ease and arts. How maddeningly richly associated by sound nearly everything in the poem is to nearly everything else still had not fully asserted itself. And it was not until preparing my notes for this essay that the full significance of what I was playing with became clear.

The charts that follow Chart #1 are merely some of my charts, some of the charts that might be made. I take up the matter of the "er" words in Chart #2. Originally I had wanted to plot words like "outer," "whosoever," "bigger," "number," and "ever," but a poem like "The Sound of Trees," a poem more self-consciously a sound poem, offers many, many more, and so I looked instead for the "r" family, where "r" in combination with a vowel, not just the "e ," made a sound you could hear throughout the poem. My family of sound words grew to include "birch" and "forth" and "dares" and "air" and "fair" and "first" and "there" and "were" and "or" and even "perhaps" and "entirely." Of the 177 total words in the poem, 25 of them are "r" words of this type. Then, because I was working with vowels I thought about making separate charts for each word as dominated by a given vowel sound. There are few "u" words in the poem. But that still leaves me four others. Because both "i" and "e" are strong in the first lines I did these charts. I enclose as #3 the one I did for the "i." Forty words of the 177 turn out to be "i" words. That is a very large number, I think, given the fact that of the connective words, incidentals like conjunctions and prepositions and especially definite and indefinite articles, which might be expected to appear in large numbers, only a few of these would normally contain an "i." "The" and "a" and "and" do not. The pronoun "it," however, does. And it is "it" we hear (or "its") quite often in these lines.

Chart 2
"r" and any vowel preceding an "r"

The birch begins to crack its outer sheath
Of baby green and show the white beneath,
As whosoever likes the young and slight
May well have noticed. Soon entirely white
To double day and cut in half the dark
It will stand forth, entirely white in bark,
And nothing but the top a leafy green—
The only native tree that dares to lean,
Relying on its beauty, to the air.
(Less brave perhaps than trusting are the fair.)
And someone reminiscent will recall
How once in cutting brush along the wall
He spared it from the number of the slain,
At first to be no bigger than a cane,
And then no bigger than a fishing pole,
But now at last so obvious a bole
The most efficient help you ever hired
Would know that it was there to be admired,
And zeal would not be thanked that cut it down

Greg Kuzma

When you were reading books or out of town.
It was a thing of beauty and was sent
To live its life out as an ornament.

Note: In "hired" and others it is the "re" which is sounded.

I began to make many charts. I latched on to the "b" words, prominent with "birch" and "baby" and "begins," and found other key words, thematic words, if you will, like "beauty" and "brave." I also found the always-awkward word for me— "bole"—in line 16. I began to formulate the theory that the prominence of "b" words, where the sound is strongly asserted but without any awkwardness helped resolve the disturbance that might be occasioned by using such an odd word as "bole" to rhyme with. Maybe it was with "bole" and how I tried to understand how sound ameliorated for me my resistance to it that alerted me to the fact that sound is not just a game in the

Chart 3
The "i" family

The birch begins to crack its outer sheath
Of baby green and show the white beneath,
As whosoever likes the young and slight
May well have noticed. Soon entirely white.
To double day and cut in half the dark
It will stand forth, entirely white in bark,
And nothing but the top a leafy green—
The only native tree that dares to lean,
Relying on its beauty, to the air.
(Less brave perhaps than trusting are the fair.)
And someone reminiscent will recall
How once in cutting brush along the wall
He spared it from the number of the slain,
At first to be no bigger than a cane,
And then no bigger than a fishing pole,
But now at last so obvious a bole
The most efficient help you ever hired
Would know that it was there to be admired,

> And zeal would not be thanked that cut it down
> When you were reading books or out of town.
> It was a thing of beauty and was sent
> To live its life out as an ornament.

poem, not just a surface distraction, but that it is working just as hard as those words that go together to create an image of the tree as "young" and "slight," a gentle unassuming thing, an innocent trusting thing.

In making up the "i" chart, I learned to distinguish between long and short "i," especially since I was hearing short "i" to begin with, but then from "white" and "like" and "slight" out to the rhyme of "slight" and "white" the other sound took over. The "i" chart began to fascinate me. If "A Young Birch" derives some of its necessary tension from the struggle of the birch to reveal its true color, its true whiteness, a struggle it makes against itself which is, significantly, what all the "young and slight" must do in their growing up—then the little civil war going on between long and short "i" is, in effect, metaphoric of that tension. Indeed, for the first six lines, the whole section where the cracking of the sheath is in progress, the distribution of warring "i" sounds is all but even, eight short, seven long. Afterwards, after the whiteness establishes itself, the war over, one "i" sound dominates the rest of the poem. Of 26 words using the "i" all but four use one sound, and one of these four also uses the other too.

The problem with my theory though is that although long "i" is the sound of the word "white," the triumphant color, Frost finds the short "i" much more useful in detailing the rest of the poem. Does this mean the seeming relationship between sound and meaning is delusional? Perhaps. Or does it mean that the game is more subtle than this? I was just about ready to give up when I noticed another equation in which to express the struggle. What we have here is not, after all, "white" fighting "white," but "white" antagonistic to "green," the "baby green" of line two. Of the first two lines's 20 syllables, five express the long "e" sound of "green." Lines 1 through 4 are also strong in "i" sounds, both short and long, and in these lines and in five and six, where the whiteness takes over, the long "e" of

"green" all but disappears. We hear it only in the last syllable
of "entirely" in line 4. It is only after "white" has dominated
the trunk, the bark, and "green" shifted upwards towards the
leaves, "the top a leafy green," that the sound returns. In the
whole long speculation/recollection of lines 11 through 20,
where Frost reminisces on how such trees may get accidentally
saved from hired help, there are only five expressions of the
long "e" sound amongst seventeen of the "i" sound. If this is
play, as well it may be, it is play of a serious sort.

The sound of "i" then is a dominant sound. Forty of the
177 words. Only a few small words, "its" outstanding, many
two-syllable words, and most nearly all of the large words.
"Reminiscent" has the "i" twice, "efficient" also, though the
second "i" makes the long "e" sound instead. (There is a lot
of play on visual resemblance and eye-rhyme in this poem,
which I will not go into.) Of words longer than two syllables
only three, "whosoever," "obvious," and "ornament" are not
controlled by the "i." Of these three, "ornament" struck me as
being quite important as the last and final word of the poem,
and also as what seemed to be the one place Frost commits
himself to finding another term for how to sum up the being
and function of the mature tree. Metaphor, in other words, or
simile. Is there anything usually more important in Frost?

And so one of my next charts was the "n" family,
being that "n" appears twice in "ornament," and being that
"ornament" is the final word of the poem "n" achieves special
status. Suddenly, with the "n," I uncovered a bonanza. 52 of
177 words are "n" words. "Begins" and "green" and "soon"
and "stand" and "nothing" and "native and "trusting" and
"cutting" and "number" and "slain" "cane" "fishing" "efficient"
"know" "thanked" "reading" "thing" along with all the ands
and ons and ones and whens. And "ornament." There is no
line in which an "n" word does not appear. Furthermore, words
containing "n" contribute mightily to the rhyme pairings. Of
the eleven couplets, four pairs contain "n": green/lean; slain/
cane; down/town; and sent/ornament. Clearly I had stumbled
upon a rich vein of sound.

This is the kind of work it is then. I had had no idea "n"
was going to prove to be so important to the poem. The "i"

sound had seemed important enough. "L" had interested me for a while in that "slight" and "entirely" stood out for me in their lines, but the "l" chart showed the sound no more than reasonably distributed. Working close, as I was, underlining and circling, but still missing letters or sounds, I began to feel like someone studying slides under a microscope, looking for that one medium in which cell growth was spectacular, or looking for strange mysterious interrelationships among things which, even if they are not actively transforming themselves as we watch, may be even harder to see because they are so familiar, so much a given part of our reality that we never look at them or listen to them. The look/listen problem also was a factor. I could hear things in the poem, or thought I heard things, I then couldn't find. Or what I heard seemed beautifully rich and intricate but then, when I consulted the text, I was not able to locate exactly or account for fully where the energy, the beauty, was coming from. Why was "double day" so fresh and bold in my ears? Certainly not because it names a book publishing company. Why did "stand forth" stand forth so proudly in the lines? Why did the breeze seem to be alive at the top of the tree in its "leafy green"? What is especially gorgeous about line 10—"Less brave perhaps than trusting are the fair"? Why did the sounds of these words seem all but to detach themselves from the worldly duty of their meanings and soar toward the airy heaven of unearthly music? Such things reminded me of

Chart 4
The "n" family
vowels in combination with "n," and "n" in initial positions

> The birch begins to crack its outer sheath
> Of baby green and show the white beneath,
> As whosoever likes the young and slight
> May well have noticed. Soon entirely white
> To double day and cut in half the dark
> It will stand forth, entirely white in bark,
> And nothing but the top a leafy green—
> The only native tree that dares to lean,
> Relying on its beauty, to the air.

(Less brave perhaps than trusting are the fair.)
And someone reminiscent will recall
How once in cutting brush along the wall
He spared it from the number of the slain,
At first to be no bigger than a cane,
And then no bigger than a fishing pole,
But now at last so obvious a bole
The most efficient help you ever hired
Would know that it was there to be admired,
And zeal would not be thanked that cut it down
When you were reading books or out of town.
It was a thing of beauty and was sent
To live its life out as an ornament.

the strange experience of hearing Frost read "An Old Man's Winter Night" where I heard distinctly, though Frost read with sharp and precise enunciation, "cracker branches" (whatever strange wonder they were) instead of "crack of branches," and wondered if I'd ever know what possibly "nothing so like beating on a box" might mean. Or in hearing "Never Again Would Birds' Song Be the Same," hearing "choral laughter" in place of "call or laughter"—what is typed so otherwise in the text, but to this very moment having had to look it up, expecting to be telling you the opposite of what I've just said. Is this what it means to have a good ear? Is this what the poet writes whose ear detects in the sounds of wind and songs of birds almost the human cry? Why all the wonderful poems in Frost's work about sounds. Or, perhaps even more idiosyncratic, why write a poem about how something looks and how its looks change and grow more lovely to our eyes and express this growth not in images and details which are such profuse opportunities in our language but instead as a symphony of sounds, an elaborate musical composition the more elaborate the more one tries to find the shape of or end of it. "Plainly with an intelligence I dealt"—the line from Frost's own microscopic study of that "considerable speck" leapt into consciousness in an ecstatic moment of epiphany.

Does one imagine feet beneath the living mite? Does one carve in marble eyebrows, eyelashes, even though they can't be seen except by someone kissing it? Does one write music in honor of Spring's deluge of sound by writing in a piccolo to voice a little bird? A part for a drop of rain? And let the bird sing even as the storm's thunder nearly entirely obscures it with drums.

Working on the charts, it's easy to lose touch with larger patterns. Or to forget the purpose behind undertaking the work to begin with. I am trying to show a texture of related sounds, how much there exists an interlocking or interweaving of patterns so that each discrete element is bound within the overall work, and yet seems free and uninhibited and loose at the same time. Bound, but "loosely bound/ By countless silken ties of love and thought." Will Frost's brilliant self-reflective "A Silken Tent" serve as a gloss to the uncelebrated "A Young Birch?" That would be truly ironic.

The "s" sound, and soft "c" are profuse in the opening four lines, and then become more or less part of the general random assortment we usually get. Where they are profuse, however, they seem to carry what the "s" typically carries, a sense of movement, motion, restlessness, energy. Because the "s" is found in "its"—an important word—"s" becomes identified with the restless growing of the tree. Because "s" is always such a common letter it helps keep the tree alive all the way through the poem, right into the last two lines:

> It was a thing of beauty and was sent
> To live its life out as an ornament.

Soft "c" goes with the "s," but hard "c" (or "k") sounds as in "crack" and "likes" and "cut" in the first five lines work to present the crackling growth of the emerging tree. These sounds are made the more physical by being always in verbs. Birch trees do not grow fast, but this one's growth is speeded up enormously through Frost's long familiarity with it as expressed in a poem that takes only a minute or so to read. As well the verbal strength of "crack" and "cut" carries over into "likes," making it more preferential and committed than it might otherwise be. Measured against "love" it would be weak. Frost may be going out of his way to be reasonable, although he usually is anyway. One can "like" beauty, he is saying—you don't have to love it. But if you do so it may then often be no more than the beauty of young things, the little calf in "The Pasture," the most famous example, or the colt in "The Runaway." We are not encouraged to waste a lot of worry on the runaway, what Frost would call "wrong sympathy"—it must

Chart 5
The "s" sound (and soft "c")
the "t" sound

The birch begins to crack its outer sheath
Of baby green and show the white beneath,
As whosoever likes the young and slight
May well have noticed. Soon entirely white.
To double day and cut in half the dark
It will stand forth, entirely white in bark,
And nothing but the top a leafy green—
The only native tree that dares to lean,
Relying on its beauty, to the air.
(Less brave perhaps than trusting are the fair.)
And someone reminiscent will recall
How once in cutting brush along the wall
He spared it from the number of the slain,
At first to be no bigger than a cane,
And then no bigger than a fishing pole,
But now at last so obvious a bole
The most efficient help you ever hired
Would know that it was there to be admired,
And zeal would not be thanked that cut it down
When you were reading books or out of town.
It was a thing of beauty and was sent
To live its life out as an ornament.

learn about winter. But we would do well to "like" the "young and slight" and provide for them.

"T" words interested me too, partly because the "t" sound is all that's left from "its" that is uncharted, because it, too, is a common sound, and also because it features in our important word "ornament." The "s" words are prolific enough, but in chart 5, I show both "s" and "t." I want to begin working toward the ultimate goal, as stated, to show the interweaving of all the various elements. In charting the "t," however, I omit where "t" is part of the "th" sound, which is really a different sound altogether. Chart 5 then is the first of many possible overlap charts. In it the poem begins to look crowded. I leave to your imagination what the poem would look like were I to add underlining for the many "n" words, and were I to add the incidence of just one vowel, the "i." The poem is beginning to reveal a density of certain sounds and a paucity of other sounds. Long "a" for example, which is such a common sound to rhyme pairs in Frost, and which ends two pairs of couplets here, is really quite scarce. I make a special chart for the long "a," not because it is important, but because it is relatively unimportant. Chart 6 shows its scattered occurrences. And yet its contribution is not merely quantitative. Where it does occur it appears as the dominant vowel sound in a stressed syllable, once as the crucial verb "spared," and four times as final couplet rhymes. Charting it on the page it does seem to follow a descending pattern from left to right as we read down, and ultimately disappears before we get into the last four lines. This displacement of the sound is one of the little secret internal movements of the poem. I'm not sure this slow shift of the "a" outward and through the poem to where it fades out completely is something we are conscious of, but it is the sort of curious phenomenon such analyses can't help but wonder at. Perhaps it gets subliminally associated with things that don't stay, some of those "number of the slain" that are lost to us, and against which the survival of the one birch makes a reminder, a marker, an index. Frost's choice of "ornament" begins to acquire some unexpected resonance within such a context.

Chart 6
The scattered contribution of the long "a" sound

The birch begins to crack its outer sheath
Of baby green and show the white beneath,

As whosoever likes the young and slight
May well have noticed. Soon entirely white.
To double day and cut in half the dark
It will stand forth, entirely white in bark,
And nothing but the top a leafy green—
The only native tree that dares to lean,
Relying on its beauty, to the air.
(Less brave perhaps than trusting are the fair.)
And someone reminiscent will recall
How once in cutting brush along the wall
He spared it from the number of the slain,
At first to be no bigger than a cane,
And then no bigger than a fishing pole,
But now at last so obvious a bole
The most efficient help you ever hired
Would know that it was there to be admired,
And zeal would not be thanked that cut it down
When you were reading books or out of town.
It was a thing of beauty and was sent
To live its life out as an ornament.

Another sound that seems to show movement over the overall living complex of the poem is the "th" sound. Something really spectacular accompanies its movement, something worthy of being called an evolution. "Th" is of course common in the poem for all the definite articles we can't help but have. Hardly ever, however, is "the" an important word. Frost's making its accidental appearance in "The Sound of the Trees" almost a Federal case suggests that he himself was not careless with it, and yet in all the early lines of "A Young Birch," "the" is almost entirely unvoiced, nearly always the downside of the iambic sine curve—"The birch," "the white," "the young," and so on. But the "th" is loud, however, in the first pair of rhymes, "sheath" and "beneath." Here the "th" sound may be said to be buried within the words, although prominent because they are end-stressed syllables. Twice more we get the buried "th" in the first seven lines, in "forth" and "nothing." The phrase "stand forth" is especially provocative. The "s" and "t" combine here for the first (and last!) time in the poem, the combination without precedent, and which does not become a precedent. "Stand forth" serves as a turning point, where the birch, no longer concealing itself in green, displays its full and true self. The rest of the word, the "and" part, is interesting too. We have come to the end of "and show the white" and "young and slight," where the sound "and" is about as inconspicuous as they come. Now the sound rallies into action. "And" the conjunction, the passive link, combines with the "st" sounds to forge the formidable verb. "Forth" is part of the power too because it is not merely an adverb showing how or what degree but is an integral unit in the infinitive "to stand forth." Up to this point there is no "or" sound combination in the poem, and so in "forth" it contributes a sudden freshness of sound comparable to a sudden blare of the trumpet. Befitting this glorious occasion the iambic sway of the earlier lines suddenly bunches and crests: "It will stand forth," with three syllables in a row all taking and releasing energy. It might be said that the poem climaxes here, becoming quiet afterwards, so quiet that line 10 ("Less brave perhaps than trusting are the fair.") is almost inaudible. But the "th" sound, once concealed, like the bright white undeniable bark of the birch, is now released, and, thereafter, in the remaining lines, occupies only lead-off positions, launches itself another splendid career, to culminate in the strange and wonderful expression "thing of beauty" in the penultimate line. A "that," "than" twice, then another "than," another "that," among many, many "the"s, and "then," as if in finale, the strongly-stressed "there," the even-more strongly-stressed "thanked," and finally "thing of beauty," ornament, loveliest of trees. More importantly, the evolution of the "th" sound matches and parallels and expresses and metaphors the growing emergence to maturity of the young birch to full-blown status. Chart 7 shows the process. All this talk about patterns of sound, and charting them on flat sheets, makes the poem seem much more static and passive than it is. It is not static and passive at all. It is urgent and bountiful, as these various sounds get clustered and heaped up, some building, some diminishing, as we read. It is a very dynamic process. The poem is powered throughout by Frost's patented iambic pentameter motor, really the same old reliable

motor we've used for hundreds of years, but equipped with
Robert Frost's special patented features that permit variation
and a capacity for extreme delicacy even as its torque and force
remain unimpaired.

Chart 8 shows the many strong starts Frost makes line by
line with his iambic. "Thĕ bírch," "Mǎy wéll," "Ĭt wíll," "Hǒw

Chart 7
The evolution of the "th" sound
Initial "th" and buried "th"

The birch begins to crack its outer sheath
Of baby green and show the white beneath,
As whosoever likes the young and slight
May well have noticed. Soon entirely white
To double day and cut in half the dark
It will stand forth, entirely white in bark,
And nothing but the top a leafy green—
The only native tree that dares to lean,
Relying on its beauty, to the air.
(Less brave perhaps than trusting are the fair.)
And someone reminiscent will recall
How once in cutting brush along the wall
He spared it from the number of the slain,
At first to be no bigger than a cane,
And then no bigger than a fishing pole,
But now at last so obvious a bole
The most efficient help you ever hired
Would know that it was there to be admired,
And zeal would not be thanked that cut it down
When you were reading books or out of town.
It was a thing of beauty and was sent
To live its life out as an ornament.

once," "Hĕ spáred," "Ăt fírst," "Ănd thén," "Bŭt nów," and so
on. Indeed nearly all the line starts may be forced to comply
with the meter; lines like "As whosoever" and "Of baby green"
and "And someone reminiscent" provide variation and subtlety,
that naturalness of voice Frost makes a myth in his work but

which is also really there at times. I mark in chart 8, however, only those beginnings where Frost expresses the stress pattern in terms of two monosyllabic words, and the firmness of these line starts, as well as the overall security of the iambic meter throughout the poem, makes for that firmness I mentioned early, that feeling of being swept up and along toward some important, memorable, undeniable, and inevitable conclusion.

Chart 8

Strong iambic starts

> <u>The birch </u>begins to crack its outer sheath
> Of baby green and show the white beneath,
> As whosoever likes the young and slight
> <u>May well </u>have noticed. Soon entirely white
> To double day and cut in half the dark
> <u>It will </u>stand forth, entirely white in bark,
> And nothing but the top a leafy green—
> The only native tree that dares to lean,
> <u>Relying</u> on its beauty, to the air.
> (Less brave perhaps than trusting are the fair.)
> And someone reminiscent will recall
> <u>How once </u>in cutting brush along the wall
> <u>He spared </u>it from the number of the slain,
> <u>At first </u>to be no bigger than a cane,
> <u>And then </u>no bigger than a fishing pole,
> <u>But now </u>at last so obvious a bole
> <u>The most </u>efficient help you ever hired
> <u>Would know </u>that it was there to be admired,
> <u>And zeal </u>would not be thanked that cut it down
> <u>When you </u>were reading books or out of town.
> <u>It was </u>a thing of beauty and was sent
> <u>To live </u>its life out as an ornament.

Line endings are not nearly so firmly iambic—and much of the playfulness, the lightness of the poem, derives from the complex play we get as lines turn. But there are many line ends which are strongly iambic: "bĕneáth," "thĕ dárk," "tŏ leán," "thĕ aír," "thĕ faír," "rĕcáll," (especially strong since the word itself is an iambic foot), "thĕ wáll," "thĕ sláin," "ă cáne." The ends of the last six lines introduce many variations, the most disrupting of these being the added eleventh syllables and consequent falling meters of "hirĕd" and "ădmirĕd." "Out of town" takes stress on each syllable, as does "and was sent" perhaps. The rhythm of the last four lines is noteworthy enough to show.

> Ănd zéal wŏuld nŏt bé thankĕd thăt cút ĭt dówn
> Whĕn yóu wĕre réadĭng bóoks ŏr oút óf tówn.
> Ĭt wăs ă thíng ŏf beaŭty ánd wăs sént
> Tŏ líve ĭts lífe oút ăs ăn órnămént.

I'm not totally comfortable with this scansion. Some of this can be read differently, and maybe there a number of possible variant readings here. Suffice it to say the meter of the last four lines is flexible, variable. There is one notable consistency, however, a tendency for the final three syllables in the lines to separate themselves off from the rest of the line into a compact phrasal sequence. "Cut it down," "out of town," "and was sent," "ornament." If we were working backwards it would be easy to hear how the line ends might take their lead from the fact that "ornament" is a three-syllable word, one of only two in the poem to end a line, the other one being "admired," but the only one both to begin and end in stress. "Admired" is an amphibrach, a substitution for the iambic foot which normally ends these lines. I don't know what name to call "ornament," except maybe "inverted amphibrach." What's considerably more important than naming it is seeing that "A Young Birch" is thick with these strange metric hybrids.

"Double day" is one. So is "leafy green." "Of the slain" is closer to an anapest, but it is not quite an anapest. "Will recall" is one of the strange feet. And "spared it from" and many others. As we read the poem aloud they seem to start early with "baby green," but maybe even earlier with "outer sheath" in line one. The precondition for each of these is the slightly less than normally-unstressed syllable to lead off what otherwise is an iambic pair, or an especially heavily stressed first-stressed syllable. "Double day" might almost be a dactyl. And some of these are close to being dactyls: "White in bark," "baby green," "outer sheath." Perhaps because of the rhythmic playfulness here, or what amounts to a sort of subversion posed by the trisyllabic units, reading the poem is an extremely pleasurable experience. I know of no other Frost poem in which metrical scansion is so nearly impossible, even while there is not one single place where stress falls improperly, too heavily or awkwardly. The very rhythm of the poem seems alive.

Chart 9
Three-syllable clusters in anticipation of "ornament"

/ ˘ /

The birch begins to crack its outer sheath
Of baby green and show the white beneath,
As whosoever likes the young and slight
May well have noticed. Soon entirely white.
To double day and cut in half the dark
It will stand forth, entirely white in bark,
And nothing but the top a leafy green--
The only native tree that dares to lean,
Relying on its beauty, to the air.
(Less brave perhaps than trusting are the fair.)
And someone reminiscent will recall
How once in cutting brush along the wall
He spared it from the number of the slain,
At first to be no bigger than a cane,
And then no bigger than a fishing pole,
But now at last so obvious a bole
The most efficient help you ever hired
Would know that it was there to be admired,
And zeal would not be thanked that cut it down
When you were reading books or out of town.
It was a thing of beauty and was sent
To live its life out as an ornament.

One of the earliest discoveries I made, some years ago, and which I made a lot of in class, involves work at the line ends. I had noticed in hearing the poem read and in reading it aloud that many of the rhyme sounds at the line ends seemed not especially surprising. It wasn't that I was losing my place in the poem, or that I'd forget the couplet sound over the interval, but that I was hearing some of the sounds before they occurred locked in at the line ends. It was as if they were being proposed, considered, some perhaps rejected, some postponed for a while, and others chosen. The word "dares" in line 8, of "dares to lean," offers up its vowel sound as a candidate for the next couplet, and is chosen—"air" ends line 9. This seemed altogether marvelous to me. Rhyme was not then going to be something stuck on, tacked on the ends of the lines, but was actually growing up out of the sounds of the words of the body of the poem. I went to see if this thing happened more than once. And sure enough, at the same exact position, three syllables from the line end in line two, the word "white" occurs, which then projects its sound as the rhyme sound "slight" and "white" of lines 3 and 4.

Working on down the right-hand margin, now in the light of these discoveries, a zone of unpredictable event and sure excitement, I found "leafy green" in line 7 as part of the "leafy green"/"lean" couplet. But here a variation on this pattern of projection was occurring. The "l" of "leafy," the consonant sound in this instance, was being sent forth to supplant the "gr" of "green" to create the new word "lean." This consonantal projection occurs in line 11 as well, with "will recall" creating "wall" in line 12. Something as interesting, but again different, occurs in lines 19 and 20. The shift in the rhyme word is from the "d" of "down" to the "t" of "town," and all three words preceding "down" in line 19 all end in "t." The transformation is promoted not from outside to outside or initial-stressed positions but from the insides out, the ends out. In the final line, as befitting the conclusion of a poem as richly complex as "A Young Birch," the interplay is almost beyond my power to document. Fully five words are involved at the end of line 20—"books or out of town," but even "When," the first word in the line, makes an essential contribution by providing the "en" sound for "sent." The "en" combines with the "s" of "books," and

the "t" of "that" and "cut" and "town" to make "sent." The
"out" of "out of town" returns in "life out" in the final line.
"Was" of "and was sent" drops its "w" to become "as" in
the final line—"to live its life out as"—just as "and" drops
its final "d" to make the "an" of "an ornament." The "or"
of "books or out of town" contributes its sound to the first
syllable of the final word. The second syllable of "ornament"
is "an" reversed, and the final syllable "ment" is the rhyme
sound "sent" with, for variety, not a consonant occasioned
in the immediately-surrounding context, but one that forces
us to recall, if we are reminiscent enough, all the way back to
"would know that it was there to be admired." By this time,
having been properly attuned, tuned and then even more-
finely tuned, some of us may hear, faintly, "sheath of baby"
from lines 1 and 2 transformed into "thing of beauty" in line 21.

As rich and thick with sound as the end of the poem is
there is no pronounced sense of climax or crescendo. There
is even the almost opposite sort of feeling, of everything
fitting so smoothly and properly together in perfect balance
and proportion that the language of the end of the poem
seems almost modest. The word "ornament," which might
have stood out for its very inextravagance, as regarding
meaning—a tree that is ornamental is somehow less an
actual tree and more an image of a tree—becomes altogether
natural under the circumstances. Circumstances means, of
course, more in this poem than dramatic circumstances—
"ornament" is also textural, a textural event within the larger
texture of the fabric of interwoven sounds.

The inextricable interwrapping of threads of sound, and
the very tightness of the pattern, create a surface consistency
which thereby lacks any strong sense of foreground and
background. So the birch tree, which might have been
outstanding visually against certain contrasting settings, is
made to blend in without disturbance. It is all part of some
larger scheme, some, if you will, overall design, something
like a landscaping of a yard in New England. Frost is not
diminishing its beauty by any means. The light thrown off by
the tree may be said to permeate the whole poem, giving it
its light and delicate and airy atmosphere. But the whiteness

of the tree is no longer a philosophical issue. It is no dark whiteness of "design of darkness to appall," or whiteness of purity, or "blanker whiteness of benighted snow/With no expression, nothing to express," or any other symbolic whiteness. Instead of throwing the whiteness back at us as a problem, Frost has instead absorbed it, accepted it, and then defused it within the poem, refracted the bright white light into the spectrum of multicolored sounds just as the whiteness of the tree is accepted into the overall harmony of landscape.

For all my talk of the many patterns of sound, I still don't feel that I have made a convincing case. But the matter of the overall integration of sound is huge—there really are endless permutations and combinations. Memorability, or memorizability, increases always where sounds are linked and blended so that the statement of one sound is projected into the sounds of words that follow, and where the rhythm is seductive and lures the reader onward. The iambic pulse of the poem is demonstrably powerful, as is the grouping tendency into those three-syllable prototypes for "ornament." The tension that is induced as between the iambic drive and the clustering pattern is an especially important force because what results when the two interact is a forward movement, left to right, and a nearly equal reactive force, a resistant force, which somewhat impedes the flow of the iambic in its instinct to back up the flow and hold and contain sound through an even-stronger stressing than the iambic affords. As a result, the poem becomes filled with small intervals of silence, pregnant pauses in which the ear adjusts itself to what has occurred, remembers, if you will, and gathers itself up as the iambic flow takes over again so firmly to begin the new line. Each line then offers a little study time to let the sounds just preceding sink in a bit, and, because so nearly all of the words of the poem are projections, in sound, to other words, each line's words preview and anticipate the sounds to come. The poem becomes then a sort of infinitely endless series of rehearsals and performances all in one. In one line of the poem, a long "i" sound is being introduced, the long "e" vowel, introduced earlier, is getting played, while the "th" consonant sound is in happy tension between outer and inner states of being, even as other consonant sounds are martialing and mixing. The mixing of vowels with consonants compounds the complexity. Long "e" in lines 1 and 2, for example, couples with "b," then "sh," then "gr," and then "n" which themselves then go on to combine with other vowels, the "b" of "begins" becomes the "b" of "baby" (while still functioning in this word's second syllable as the "b" of "by"), the "sh" of "sheath" couples with "ow" to make "show" in line 2, the "n" of "beneath" goes on in lines 7 and 8 to join with other vowels in "nothing" and "native," while the "gr" remains bound only to the long "e" sound of "green," making but one more appearance in the poem as the rhyme word in line 7. Lines 7, 8, and 9, to take any three lines at random, reveal a complexity as stunning as what is to be found in the final lines of the poem:

> And nothing but the top a leafy green—
> The only native tree that dares to lean,
> Relying on its beauty, to the air.

"Nothing" and "native" are both two-syllable words starting with "n," and are both trochaic feet. The syllables "on" of "only" and the "on" of "on" are as if slant rhymes of each other. The three "l" words in these lines are really, in fact, "long e" words—"leafy," "only," and "leans," while the already-discussed projection of the "l" of leafy onto the rhyme word "lean" also has its complementary "fadeout" transition as "l" combines with long "i" in "Relying" in line 9. Further fadeout occurs as we follow the "l" into line 10 where it initiates the line as "Less." The assonance on long "a" of "native" and "dares" projects the new rhyme word "air" in line 9. Then there are more-subtle things, still, however, within the appreciative range of the ear. "Only" and "leafy" (both trochaic feet) rhyme on their second syllables, though they are not at line ends. Indeed, the three lines are filled with long "e" sounds if you add in "beauty" in line 9 and "tree" in line 8, and then the rhyme words "green" and "lean." There is also a stripping away of the "r" from "tree" to produce the "ty" of "beauty," followed by the restoration of the "r" in the next line to make the "tr" of "trusting." Also "but the top" and "to the air," like many combinations of words bridged by the definite article, match metrically, and maintain the definite article as a sort of fulcrum between the two weights of their stresses. Suffice it to say that as one moves outwards from these three lines, both forward and backward, the linkages compound, couplings become triplings and further, sounds that are singular over a few lines are doubled, consonantal clusters of three or four or five instances become veritable constellations, assonantal brooks swell into full-fledged rivers. Regarding the three lines in question here, the seemingly-naked second syllable of "native" which has no predecessor sound of "iv" earlier, and which seems like it will not achieve any pairing or echo in the poem, does finally link up with "live" in the very last line. By this time, if we are reading closely, or if we have been drawn back to the poem over and over again for the experience of this richness, no two points in the poem can be too far removed from each other that some perceptible energy does not flow between them. And so the fabric of the language becomes electric.

Rapid shifts of attention, yet a sustained memory and hearing, strong forward movement combined with a tugging resistance and consequent backflow, rehearsal to performance to rehearsal to performance to rehearsal again, sounds being assembled and disassembled, played, played out, renewed again or finally exhausted, statement, counter statement, synthesis, antithesis, voice-echo-voice-echo and re-echo—whatever the metaphors chosen to express this passion of sound, each seems on its own inadequate, while all of them together make for far too clumsy a mix to attribute to what in our hearing is so splendidly graceful and seemingly without effort. And yet there is provided for us an easy way to sum it all up. This is, quite simply, as they say, what it is to have a "good ear."

CPSIA information can be obtained at www.ICGtesting.com
Printed in the USA
LVOW08s0532170614

390352LV00001B/2/P